Analyzing Performance Problems

or You Really Oughta Wanna

Second Edition

Robert F. Mager
Peter Pipe

Lake Publishing Company
Belmont, California

BOOKS BY ROBERT F. MAGER

Preparing Instructional Objectives, *Revised Second Edition*

Measuring Instructional Results, *Second Edition*

Analyzing Performance Problems, *Second Edition*
(with Peter Pipe)

Goal Analysis, *Second Edition*

Developing Attitude Toward Learning, *Second Edition*

Making Instruction Work

Developing Vocational Instruction
(with Kenneth Beach)

Troubleshooting the Troubleshooting Course

ISBN-1-56103-336-7

Library of Congress Catalog Card Number: 93–60498
Printed in the United States of America

2.9

Contents

Preface

Solutions to problems are like keys in locks; they don't work if they don't fit. And if solutions aren't the right ones, the problem doesn't get solved.

This book is about problems that arise because people aren't doing what they are supposed to be doing or what you would like them to be doing. It describes each of a series of questions to ask when faced with this sort of "performance problem," and offers a quick-reference checklist to help you determine what sort of solution is most likely to work.

If you have ever been told, or have said, "We've got a training problem," or "They could do it if they wanted to," this book will help.

0 ‖ Considering the Whole

People don't do things for zillions of the darnedest reasons, leading to all sorts of problems. And when there *are* problems—caused by differences between what people do and what someone wants them to do—the common solutions are to inform or exhort, or both. You may say, "I've got to teach them . . . ," or proclaim, "They really must change their attitudes. . . ." But people problems come in many guises. They are solved by different remedies. And the one who is best at analyzing the nature of the problem will be more successful at solving it.

You're in the presence of the kind of problem we're talking about when you hear statements such as:

"They're not doing it the way they're supposed to."

"They don't have the right attitude."

"Absenteeism is too high."

"We need a course to teach people to. . . ."

"We've got a training problem because our workers aren't safety conscious."

"My sales reps don't sell our products."

"We've got to teach our students to turn in their assignments on time."

"I don't know why my kids don't mind like they oughta."

It's a mistake to assume that the answer to any of these problems necessarily involves either information or exhortation. (And usually it's an even worse mistake to assume that transfer or termination—the standard solution of so many supervisors—is automatically the answer.)

1

The trouble with all statements of the kind we've listed is that what people identify as "the problem" often isn't the problem at all. It is merely a symptom of the problem. Until the problem is understood in greater detail, proposing a solution is simply shooting from the hip.

Analyzing Performance Problems is about how to find solutions to problems of human performance. Sometimes the solution is to provide information; if someone doesn't know how to perform, instruction is likely to help. But when that person does know how and still doesn't perform, you can teach or exhort until your socks fall off and not solve the problem.

In this book, we describe a procedure for analyzing and identifying the nature and cause of these human performance problems. We will give you a series of questions for each step of the analysis, and also provide a quick-reference checklist to help you determine which solution is most likely to work. Once familiar with the procedure, you will find it quick and easy to use. Not only that, but you may find yourself with a new problem—learning to tolerate what you will be able to see quite plainly (like a person with X-ray vision) are expensive misfits between existing problems and solutions.

Flow Diagram

We will describe the steps of the procedure one by one (how else?); and, so that you can see the sequence of steps and also keep track of where you are, we will center our discussion around a flow diagram (opposite). That calls for a cautionary note, though. The flow diagram makes it look as if everything is neatly welded into place and that each step leads inevitably to the next. *Don't be deceived by appearances. The formula is not rigid.* Some of the steps logically belong in the sequence we have depicted. Others are not so related, notably those on the right-hand side of the diagram. They are shown in what looks like a sequence simply because we can talk about only one thing at a time. When you come to apply them, you may find that you can leap a step or two and go directly to the solution.

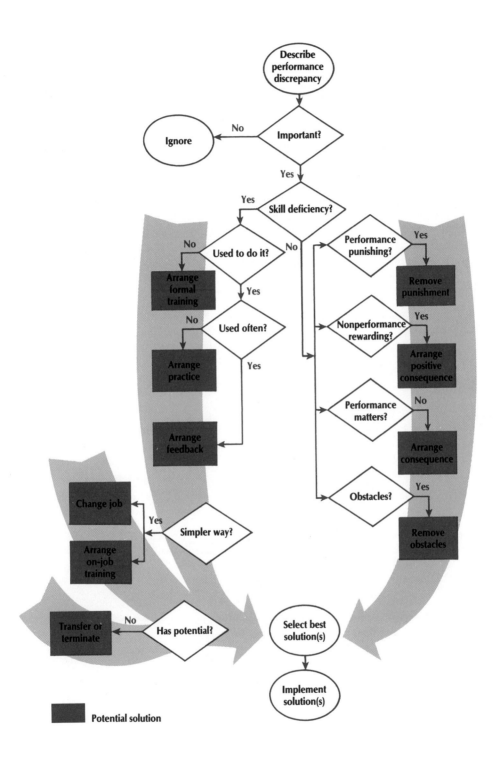

The intuitive leap is fine. In fact, our whole approach is designed to tap your serendipity button as often as possible. That leads to yet another note of caution, however: *beware the hazards of considering only one possible solution to any problem*. That's only one stage better than viewing all performance discrepancies as problems of training or attitude. To avoid this trap, you'll find the flow diagram and the checklist of questions in Part V useful. Run your problem through all the steps before you decide that your analysis is complete.

PART

I

They're Not Doing What They Should Be Doing.

I Think I've Got a Training Problem.

The procedure we are about to describe is one that shows you how to analyze the nature, the importance, and the cause of things called *performance discrepancies.* Since you can't analyze one unless you know one when you see it, let's begin there.

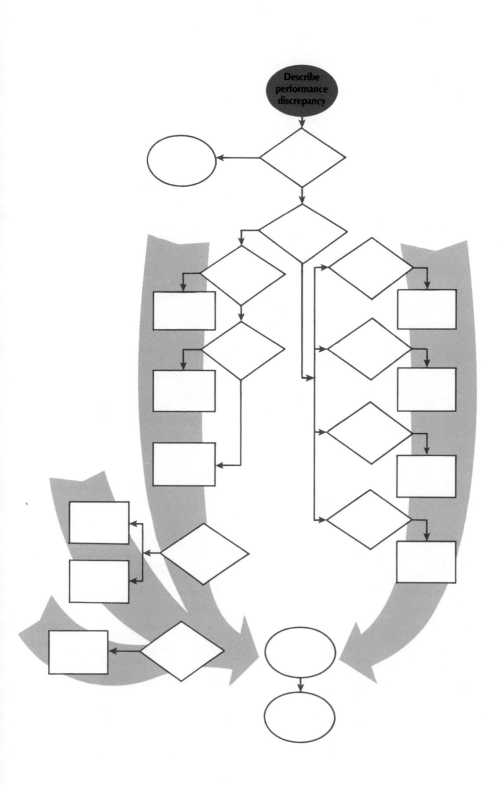

Describe
performance
discrepancy

1 | What Is the Performance Discrepancy?

Life is studded with discrepancies. There are discrepancies between what people tell you and what you know to be true, between what others believe and what you believe, between the things you want and your ability to pay— and any number of discrepancies between what *is* and what you would like it to be. One such discrepancy is that between people's *actual* performance and the performance *desired* of them. This is a performance discrepancy, the kind of discrepancy with which we will be working.

Examples of performance discrepancies can be found all around you. Sometimes you get too little, sometimes too much. There's the typist who doesn't type accurately enough to suit you, the secretary who organizes your schedule to the point of bossiness; there's the son or daughter who doesn't wash the family car as often as promised, the mechanic who sells you an unneeded oil change; and there are the members of the congregation who don't show up regularly enough to suit the minister and the woman who is unnecessarily bossy with the altar guild.

Many of these discrepancies need not exist. Many of them can be eliminated.

As we stated in our Preface, one common occurrence that warns you that a performance discrepancy may be lurking around is the announcement that takes some form of "We've got a training problem." Someone has detected a difference between what is desired and what is actually happening.

But statements such as "We've got to train/teach . . . " are pits into which one can pour great amounts of energy and money unproductively. Such statements talk about *solutions,* not *problems.* Training (teaching, instruction) is a solution, a remedy—a procedure used to achieve desired results. It implies transferring information to change someone's state of knowing or ability to perform.

But lack of information is often not the problem. Let's take a couple of our earlier examples:

> "We've got a training problem because our workers aren't safety conscious."

> "We've got to teach our students to turn in their assignments on time."

Workers *know* they are supposed to follow safety precautions. Kids *know* they are supposed to turn in their homework assignments on time. And when people *already know* how to do what you want them to do, further instruction is not likely to get the results you want.

When someone says, "I've got a training problem," it's like someone going to a doctor and saying, "I've got an aspirin problem." It's possible that aspirin will solve his or her problem, but aspirin is the solution, not the problem.

We are careful to use the word *discrepancy* rather than *deficiency.* "Discrepancy" means only that there is a difference, a lack of balance between the actual and the desired. "Deficiency" means that a value judgment has been made about a discrepancy and that the discrepancy is bad or in some other way unacceptable. Using the word *discrepancy,* we avoid jumping to conclusions about whether a discrepancy is good or bad; in this way we remember to ask the questions that will give us a solid fix on the importance of the discrepancy.

To recognize a performance discrepancy, ask *why* it occurred to someone to say such things as: "I've got a training problem." "We need a course." "He needs a lesson." Or: "They oughta wanna be interested." And even: "Why can't they ever get it right?"

Each of these statements is only a symptom of a performance discrepancy, not a description of one. And the first step toward eliminating one is understanding its nature. It may be that you noticed people working slower than usual or slower than you desire. It may be that children are leaving more food than you think is reasonable, or that they are using unacceptable language. It may be that someone is less accurate or less careful than desired, or it may be an action as exasperating as that discovered by the manager of a motion picture distribution house—people "splicing" film with staples and scotch tape.

You'll know you are in the presence of a performance discrepancy when you hear things like this.

"These new supervisors just aren't motivated."

"I see. Just what is it they're doing that causes you to say that?"

"Doing? It's what they *aren't* doing that's the problem."

"And what is that?"

"Well, for one thing, they aren't managing. They spend too much time running the machine they used to run before they were promoted. They shouldn't be doing that; they should be managing."

The *complaint* was about motivation, but the *event* causing the complaint had to do with time spent operating a machine.

"We've got to teach those kids to have the right attitude."

"Just what are they doing or not doing that makes you say that?"

"Why, they litter the place until you can't see the ground."

"I see. So you'd like to reduce the amount of litter?"

"We sure would."

The complaint was about attitude, but the performance discrepancy causing the complaint was a difference between what *existed* in the way of littering and what someone *wanted done* about littering. Here's one more.

"They just don't have the right attitude about their jobs."
"Who doesn't have the right attitude?"
"Our salespeople. They just won't use the sales aids that we provide them."

The complaint was about attitude, but the discrepancy had to do with not using sales aids.

It's difficult to select a course of action to fix a situation when it is described in such broad (fuzzy) terms as "attitude problem," or "training problem," or "motivation problem." You *can*, however, plan a course of action when you know that the discrepancy to be influenced is clear and specific.

The first step is to ask yourself, *"Why* do I say something is not the way it ought to be? Why do I say there is a 'training' problem? What *event* causes me to say that changes must be made?"

What to Do

Identify the nature of the discrepancy. Once its nature has been identified, the importance of the discrepancy can be considered.

How to Do It

Ask these questions:

- *Why do I think there is a training problem?*
- *What is the difference between what is being done and what is supposed to be done?*
- *What is the event that causes me to say that things aren't right?*
- *Why am I dissatisfied?*

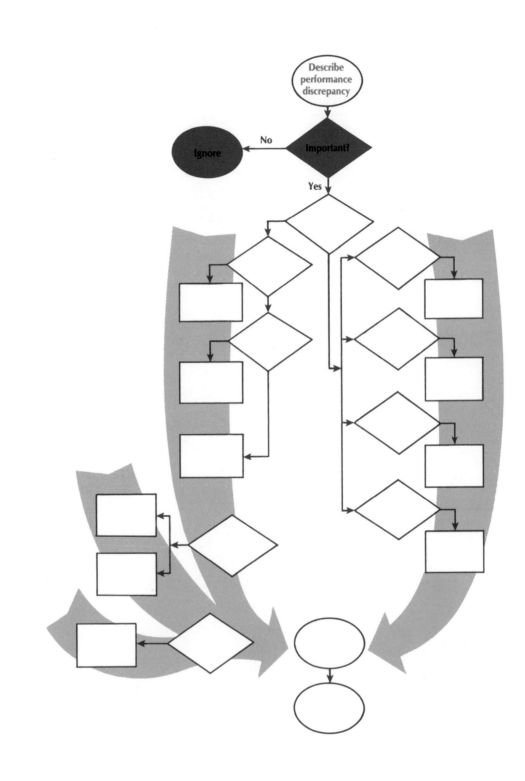

Describe performance discrepancy

Important?

No → Ignore

Yes

2 | Is It Important?

A performance discrepancy has been identified.

People see things differently. Some will perceive a joke to be the funniest thing they've ever heard, while others will wonder what the chuckling was all about. Some will perceive a sunset to be spectacular, while others will say "Ho hum." Some will consider certain behaviors to be a shocking breach of common courtesy, while others may find the same behaviors more than acceptable.

There is no question that there are different perceptions of the same event. That goes for performance discrepancies, too. Some people will feel that a particular discrepancy is urgently in need of fixing, while others will wonder what the fuss is about.

Sometime in the late 1960s, many business managers began to find a discomforting discrepancy between what they wanted and what they were getting with regard to the length of young men's hair.

"They oughta be ashamed of themselves," said these managers. "We've got to teach them not to look like women." (Translation: They really oughta wanna look like *me*.)

The discrepancy here was obvious: about three inches of hair. And it was identified and verbalized. But merely identifying a difference between what people are doing and what you would like them to be doing is *not* enough reason to take action. So, at this point in the analysis procedure, it is well to

13

ask whether the discrepancy is important enough to warrant further consideration.

When one manager was asked about the importance of this hair discrepancy, the conversation went like this:

"You are displeased with the length of the new employees' hair?"

"Yes. It is disgraceful."

"Aside from your displeasure with long-haired males, what would be the consequence of ignoring it?"

"What?"

"What would happen if you let it alone? What would happen if you ignored it?"

"Well, it probably wouldn't make much difference to business. But they ought to have more respect for the company. They ought not to want to look so sloppy."

Translated, this meant that there would be no serious consequence in terms of company success or failure. It meant only that the shorthairs would continue to be made uncomfortable by the longhairs. In such a case, it is hardly worth the trouble, and probably unwarranted, to try to remove the discrepancy.

Other companies had a different answer, however. One machine shop foreman said: "Listen, buster. Nobody in my shop wears long hair . . . or long *anything*. Guys with long hair, or long ties, or loose clothing are a hazard to themselves and to others because they can get themselves caught in the machinery."

And another manager said: "Most of our customers are shorthairs. If we send them a longhair sales rep, we just might be out of business."

In these cases there *is* a consequence of some importance, and action to eliminate the discrepancy is probably warranted.

But how to decide when to act and when to ignore? And if the decision is to act, how much action is a "cure" worth? A day? A year? And is it worth the investment of fifty dollars? A million?

For answers, you have to calculate the "size" or cost of the discrepancy. If the cost is small, the discrepancy is a good candidate for leaving alone. If it is more substantial, it may be worth some effort to consider a cure. Either way, a better decision will be made if there is more objective information about a discrepancy's importance than merely, "It's important because I thought of it first," "It's important because it irritates me," or "It's important because I say it is." So let's look at a way to evaluate the importance of a discrepancy.

In essence, what you have to do is weigh the cost of doing something about the discrepancy against the cost of doing nothing about it. Not all problems are worth the cost of the cure.

Consequences of Performance Discrepancies (Sources of Costs)

Various cost possibilities are associated with a discrepancy. There can be a direct cost in dollars, such as damaged machinery, an unacceptable amount of scrap produced (unusable product), or lost time. There can be less readily measured costs such as lost sales, increased insurance costs, or a reduction in the amount or the accuracy of work completed. There may also be "intangible" costs such as loss of goodwill, a decline in motivation to perform, or a tarnished company image. Though many of these (particularly the last) may be hard to quantify, they may be important in arriving at an objective answer. When you have your best estimate of the costs of the discrepancy, you will know not only how important it is to eliminate, but also how much time and money a solution is worth.

But be sure to analyze only the *actual* costs rather than results that someone *guesses* might be incurred by the discrepancy. It is risky to guess that this or that discrepancy *may* lead to costs. In a paper mill, for example, workers were exhorted to replace the covers on fast-moving pulleys after working on them. But they weren't replacing them, and management said, "That's one of our problems. They should be putting the covers back on, but they don't. And that's dangerous. Could lead to serious accidents."

It *could*. But when the files were checked it was found that in the entire history of the company, not a single accident had been attributed to this "discrepancy." The workers simply were more competent than they were being given credit for (as is often the case). What was the "cost" of this discrepancy?

When calculating costs, make sure you are dealing with real consequences of a performance discrepancy rather than with maybe's. Here are some likely sources of costs.

Money.   Is money lost directly (as when tellers or sales-clerks give out more money in change than they should)? Are goods or materials lost (as through theft or accident)? Calculate the amount lost per year or the amount that would be lost per year if the discrepancy were allowed to persist.

Time.   Do people waste time as a result of the discrepancy? Do they lose time because of materials shortages or lateness, because services are slow, or because defective work has to be redone? Is time lost because you or someone else worries about the discrepancy? If so, calculate the amount of time lost and its cost for a whole year.

Material Waste (Scrap).   Is more scrap generated than is acceptable? How much more? What is the value of that scrap? What's the annual cost of having it hauled away, or burned, or remelted?

Equipment Damage.   What is the cost of equipment damage resulting from the discrepancy? What's your estimate of the annual cost if the discrepancy continues?

Amount of Work Completed.   Is there less production because of the discrepancy? What's the cost of the difference between the amount of completed work you are getting and the amount you should be getting?

Accuracy of Work Completed.   Is the quality of the work suffering because of the discrepancy? How? And how much is it costing?

Insurance Premiums. Has the discrepancy led to increases in insurance premiums (as when drivers have too many accidents)? How much more per year are you paying?

Accidents. Accidents can be costly, and most of the costs can be calculated. Add up the cost of workdays lost, hospital stays, damaged or destroyed equipment, and increased insurance premiums.

Lost Business. This one may be harder to quantify, but if someone says that a discrepancy is resulting in lost business, it is fair for you to ask "How much?" The answer may be only an approximation based on a review of sales records, but even an estimate provides better guidance than a mere guess.

Does the discrepancy require customers to spend more time waiting in line, filling out forms, waiting for the doctor, or returning items for repair? (Have you noticed that since stores have installed computerized checkout terminals, you have to stand there longer while clerks push buttons?) If so, there is negative effect on the customer. Check to see whether the impact is resulting in lost business.

Duplicated Effort. Does it now take two people to do what one did before the discrepancy occurred? Are two departments now doing what only one did before? How much is that duplication costing?

Extra Supervision. Does the discrepancy mean that more supervision is needed than before? Do you need more guards, more security equipment, more monitoring time, or more monitoring equipment? Does someone spend more time overseeing?

When you have located and listed every result or consequence of the performance discrepancy, whatever the consequence's source, calculate as best you can the annual cost of each consequence. When you add all costs together you will have quantified the total cost of the discrepancy and assessed its importance. Even though you may not be able to put a dollar amount on each of the costs, you will have a reasonably objective basis for deciding (a) whether the discrepancy is worth doing something about, and (b) if so, how much you can reasonably invest in a solution.

Here are some examples.

A supervisor, complaining about the amount of rework that had to be done by her 12 typists, calculated that about 25 percent of the working day was spent redoing incorrect work. When asked how much that was costing, she replied:

"Let's see. They get an average of $12 an hour, wages and benefits. If each typist spends two hours a day on corrections, that's 24 working hours per day, or 120 hours per week. Times $12 is roughly $1,500 per week."

"And on an annual basis?"

"If we figure a 48-week year, that would be about $72,000. Wow!"

"What else happens as a result of the rework?"

"Some of the work gets delivered late, and I get chewed on by the managers who are waiting for it."

"Anything else?"

"Well, I have to spend most of my lunch hour checking the work, marking priorities, and then getting it back to the right person for rework."

"How much would that cost if you had to hire someone else to do that?"

"Hmm. At about an hour per day, or roughly 250 hours per year, that would cost the company about $3,000 or more."

"So the performance discrepancy—the difference between what you are getting and what you should be getting in the way of accuracy—is costing about $75,000 per year?"

"That's right. And that doesn't include the extra supplies and equipment maintenance costs. That probably doesn't add up to more than a few hundred dollars, but it's a real cost."

There's no question that this discrepancy was large enough to warrant action. Just what to do about such situations will be taken up in the chapters that follow.

That example points up the importance of multipliers. A single typist reworking corrections on a single day does not involve a large cost. But 12 typists, 5 days a week, 48 weeks a year, multiplies into a formidable sum.

Sometimes, if you are in the business of developing human resources, you may find yourself looking for problems to solve, rather than having an alleged "training problem" dumped on you. If at that time you find what seems to be a small problem, don't forget about multipliers.

A young man working for one of Europe's biggest supermarket chains was learning to complete this kind of analysis. The only kind of problem he could think of, he said, was too trivial to bother with. As he explained, "Each week we send out displays for the weekly loss-leader items. And as often as not, a display sits in a market's warehouse and isn't set up until a couple of days into the week."

He estimated the amount of business lost through failure to "highlight the special" to be the equivalent of $100—too little, he thought, to make an examination worthwhile.

PP: Isn't there more than one loss-leader display sent out each week?

YM: Yes. And the people in the stores are sloppy about displaying them.

PP: Every week?

YM: Yes.

PP: How many stores are affected?

YM: Several hundred.

You see the point. By the time we had multiplied all the various dimensions, this "trivial" problem was estimated to cost the equivalent of two million dollars a year!

But let's not get too pushy about the two million dollars. These were estimates, and although we tried to be conservative, perhaps the numbers were inflated. But even if the scale of the problem were only a tenth of what was estimated, that's still a lot of problem. If the true extent of the problem were only one percent of the estimate, there's still a problem worth several months of a problem-solver's time.

In Chapter 12, we will take up the question of the cost of solutions. By comparing those costs with the cost of the problem, it will be possible to make a fairly objective decision about what should be done.

Here's an example that shows it is sometimes *less* costly to *ignore* the discrepancy than to do something about it.

A sales manager with a force of more than a hundred people complained that they didn't heed his memo exhorting them to turn in a monthly article for the internal newsletter.

"I've asked each one to send in a short article each month . . . less than a page . . . describing success stories or other interesting items. But only a few of them do it."

"What happens as a result of your not getting articles from each person every month?"

"We don't hear about what they've been doing, and they don't get a chance to tell of their successes."

"How much do you suppose that's costing in terms of dollars?"

"Dollars? That's hard to say. Nothing directly, of course, but we may be losing something in terms of motivation."

"What would happen if *everyone* did as you asked?"

"What?"

"What would happen if everyone sent in an article every month?"

"Then I'd have 112 articles for the monthly newsletter . . . ahh . . . gee . . . I see I'd have to hire another typist . . . and then I'd need another word processing terminal . . . uhh . . . we'd have to add a hundred more pages to our 12-page newsletter. That's more than we can afford."

Very quickly it became clear that the cost of *eliminating* the discrepancy would have been too heavy to bear. The solution? The sales manager readjusted his expectations, and the problem evaporated.

Many discrepancies often exist only in the eyes of the beholder. They are simply personal biases about what is "right"

or a blind preference for "the way we've always done it." If you insist that a discrepancy is serious, be sure at least to ask, "Is it likely that the effort of searching for a solution will be justified by the results?"

The elimination of discrepancies can be approached from two directions. You can change what you are getting (the actual performance), or you can change your expectations (the desired performance). Or, of course, you can change both.

Changing the expectations is something that you can do on *your* side of the fence, and it may be the easiest way out. As far as the "performer" (the employee, the student, the child) is concerned, the effect is that the discrepancy has been ignored.

What to Do

Having identified a performance discrepancy that you or someone else feels is important to eliminate, be sure to find out how much the discrepancy is "costing" before taking action. To estimate the size or value (and thus the importance) of the discrepancy:

  a. *List all the consequences (outcomes) caused by the discrepancy.*

  b. *Calculate the cost of each outcome wherever possible.*

  c. *Total the costs.*

  d. *Answer the question, "What would happen if I left it alone?"*

If the result of letting it alone would be negligible, drop it there. If the result is substantially larger than nothing, go to the next steps of the analysis.

How to Do It

Ask these questions:

- *Why is the discrepancy important? (What is its cost?)*
- *What would happen if I left the discrepancy alone?*
- *Could doing something to resolve the discrepancy have any worthwhile result?*

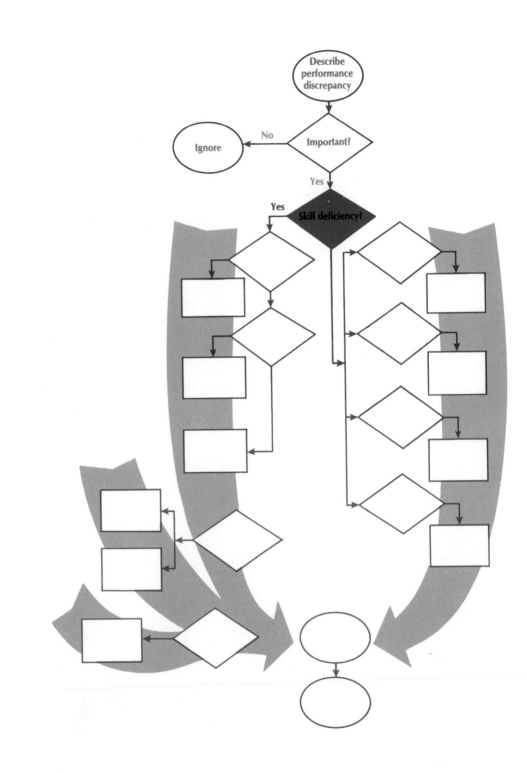

3 Is It a Skill Deficiency?

■ **WHERE WE ARE**

A performance discrepancy exists. It is considered important.

Now we begin to determine the *cause* of the discrepancy, so that an appropriate remedy can be selected or designed. This is a pivotal point in your checklist of questions, because the answer to this next question determines which of two sequences of questions you will follow.

In this step you must decide whether the performance discrepancy is due to a *skill deficiency*. In essence, are nonperformers not performing as desired because they *don't know how* to do it? If their lives depended on it, would they still not perform?

If there is a genuine skill deficiency, then the primary remedy must be either to change an existing skill level by teaching new skills or to change what people are required to do.

On the other hand, if people are able to perform but don't, the solution lies in something other than enhancement of skills. "Teaching" what is already known isn't going to change anyone's skill level. The remedy in these cases is to change the conditions under which people are expected to do that which they already know how to do.

Here are some illustrations taken from life.

The manager of a medium-sized food company says, "I've got a training problem, and I want you to develop a training program to solve it."

We ask him to explain.

"In our new plant we make only six varieties of our product; and because we have only six varieties, our sales reps travel around in panel trucks with a supply of each. In a sense, each rep is a traveling warehouse."

"And the problem?"

"The reps are pushing only *one* product instead of all six. I want you to teach them to sell all products equally."

"Do they know *how* to sell the other five?"

"Of course. It's no different from the one they are pushing."

"Do they know as much about those other five as they do about the one they're selling well?"

"Certainly they do. We have a good product course, and they have been carefully trained in all of the products."

"So they could sell the others if their lives depended on it?"

"Of course. But they don't."

"Do you have any idea why they don't push those other five products?"

"Well, yes. I suppose it's because they get three times as much commission for the one as they do for the other five. But they ought to want to sell the others *anyhow*."

Aha! What started out to be one of those "I've got a training problem" episodes turns out to be something entirely different. The performance discrepancy is clearly *not* due to a lack of skill. The sales reps *could* sell the products, but they don't. In this case, training is clearly not the remedy. What would you teach? What would you put into a course? What information could be imparted that the reps don't already have? True, you could lecture them on the importance of selling the products equally (if they don't already know that). Or you could explain how their jobs depend on their selling those other five products (if that is really true). But training will *not* make any difference in their *skill* at doing that which the manager wants them to do. Since they already know how to do as desired, the answer is not training. It's something else.

Another example: A principal says, "We've got to teach these kids not to write on the toilet walls."

Well, what would you put into a course on Non-toilet-wall Writing? Can't you just see the curriculum?

Monday. Introduction to Nonwriting

Tuesday. History of Nonwriting

Wednesday. Toilet Appreciation

Thursday. Famous Johns and Their Dastardly Defacement

Friday. Pot Power

Managers are often heard to say, "If only we could make these people more safety conscious." One interview with a manager went like this:

"Safety is a real problem for you?"

"Yes, it is. Every year we lose two million dollars because of accidents."

"Do you think your employees can recognize a safety hazard when they see one?"

"Oh, sure. Most of them have been around for some time, and they know what's safe and what isn't."

"Do they know how to report a safety hazard?"

"Yes, but they don't. And they oughta wanna do more about safety. It's in their own best interest. We need to teach them to be more safety conscious."

So the manager put safety posters on the walls and insisted that employees watch safety films regularly.

Nothing much happened to the accident rate, as might be expected, for this was another of those cases where people knew how to perform as desired but didn't. It was another of those cases where there existed an important performance discrepancy that was *not due* to a skill deficiency. In such cases the question is not what to teach, but rather how to rearrange things to get the performance that is already available.

At this point we will take a closer look at a term we will deliberately be using throughout the book—"oughta wanna." This is the key term to look for when trying to determine whether a performance discrepancy is due to a lack of skill. Whenever you hear someone say, "They oughta wanna," or some variation thereof (usually accompanied by the waggling of a forefinger), it is almost certain that you are *not* dealing with a skill deficiency. It is almost certain that the people *could* perform as desired if the conditions and the consequences were right.

- The sales reps know how to sell the products, but they don't; they oughta wanna.
- Kids oughta wanna brush their teeth without being nagged by their parents.
- George oughta wanna clean his shoes before coming into the house.

No amount of information, no amount of exhortation, is necessarily going to change an "oughta wanna" situation. What's needed is a change in the conditions or the consequences surrounding the desired performance. "You oughta wanna do it *for your own good*" is not a potent motivator; it is one of the weakest techniques known for influencing anyone to do something he or she already knows how to do.

In thinking about this issue, we wonder if the trouble doesn't spring from the imprecision with which many people so often use our language. They say things like, "I'll *teach you* to sass your mother." But this does not mean that the speaker intends to instruct the sasser in how to sass the sassee. It means that the speaker intends, through the arrangement of conditions and consequences (whap!), to modify the performance of the sasser—to cause that child to do something he or she already knows how to do; namely, to refrain from sassing.

Perhaps this explains the genesis of the expression "I've got a training problem." It seems that often when a difference is perceived between what someone is doing and what others would like that person to be doing, they conclude that the way to get the difference reduced is by training, by instruction. But training is only one of the remedies for a performance discrepancy. In fact, training is only one of the remedies *even when* a genuine skill deficiency exists.

After all, there are different "forms" of skill deficiencies. Sometimes people can't do it today because they have *forgotten* how, and sometimes because they *never knew* how. Solutions for these situations are different. And sometimes people don't do the job because they can't—perhaps they lack the mental capacity or the physical strength. Again, a different solution is called for.

Sometimes you may find it hard to judge whether a skill deficiency is involved, or how much of a deficiency it is. If records don't tell you whether the skill was once present, and you can't tell by watching people as they try to do the thing they are suspected of not doing, then you might try the direct approach. Talk to some of them and ask them whether *they* feel their skill is weak or whether something else is causing the discrepancy.

In summary, then, when you detect an important performance discrepancy, it is *not* automatically a "training problem," and the solution does not necessarily involve teaching/training. Before you can arrive at a true solution (one that works, that is), you must first discover what kind of problem you have. And the key step at this stage is to determine whether the performance discrepancy is due to a genuine skill deficiency.

We'll consider first the case in which *a skill deficiency does exist*. Part II will lead you through the appropriate path on the flow diagram. Then, in Part III, we will back up to the same choice point and describe the path followed when the skill is there but the performance is not.

What to Do

Determine whether the discrepancy is due to a genuine skill deficiency.

How to Do It

Ask these questions:

- *Could the person do it if really required to do it?*
- *Could the person do it if his or her life depended on it?*
- *Are the person's present skills adequate for the desired performance?*

PART

II

Yes. It Is a Skill Deficiency.

They Couldn't Do It if Their Lives Depended on It.

We're face to face with a genuine skill deficiency. But it still isn't time to assume that a formal training program is needed. By asking a series of questions, you can refine your understanding of why the deficiency exists and shape a solution that gets at the underlying cause.

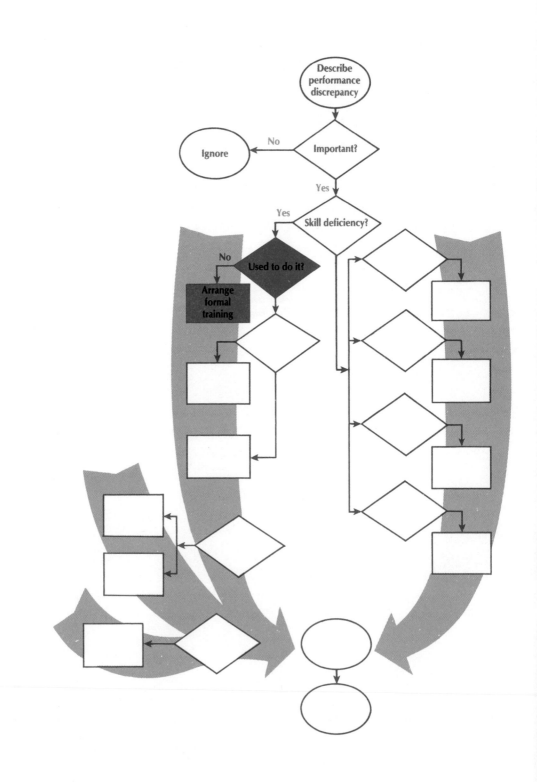

4 Could They Do It in the Past?

■ WHERE WE ARE

A performance discrepancy exists and is considered important. It has been established that it is a genuine skill deficiency.

"Shucks," said the elderly gentleman, "I used to know how to do that pretty good. You just give me a day or two to practice the kinks out and I'll be right in there with the best of 'em."

If he's right, what a waste it would be to start teaching him the skill from the very beginning. In terms of what has to be done to get rid of a skill deficiency, there's a great difference between the skill that *used to be* and the skill that *never was*. Yet the number of instances in which we make the mistake of trying to teach people something they already know is very large indeed.

So the thing to do next is ask: Could they do it in the past?

Determining whether a lack of skill is due to a form of forgetting or to a lack of training is one of the more important decisions in the analysis of performance discrepancies. It's also one of the more neglected decisions.

(Even when it's plain that a genuine skill deficiency exists and that a person has *never had* the skill, the solution is not necessarily a formal training program. This issue is explored in

Chapter 6, but it isn't too early for a cautionary note: *beware of conclusions about the existence of genuine deficiencies.* It's amazing how many courses are given under the assumption that students know nothing whatsoever about the main topic until taught otherwise. All of the students are made to wade through all of the material from the beginning. This can waste a great deal of time and may create misconceptions about the effectiveness of a course where the teacher succeeds in "teaching" what the students already knew.)

If you have ever gotten involved with children and ended up cricking your back while playing games or bending your ego as you founder over eighth-grade mathematics, you will agree that time can play havoc with skills that used to exist. It happens in jobs, too. Consider this example.

Several years ago, one of us was a member of a team assigned to assess the proficiency of radar maintenance men who had graduated from a military course designed to teach that skill. The team traveled to locations around the country to test each maintenance man on his own equipment. While the maintenance man waited outside, the team "inserted a trouble" in his radar equipment. He was then shown one symptom, much as it happens when a radar operator discovers that something isn't working.

One young man tested did an incredibly poor job, even though he had done well during his training. He hardly knew where things were located, let alone what to do to find the trouble. Here, it seemed, was a performance discrepancy of large proportions. When the results of the test were reported, as was required, his commanding officer exploded.

"Get that man in here," he roared. "I'll *teach him* to make our unit look bad."

Fortunately, he was persuaded to sit still long enough to answer a few questions.

"How long has this man been assigned to your unit?" he was asked.

"About six months."

"What has he been doing during that time?"

"He's been assigned as an oiler."

"How much time has he spent inside the radar van?"

"Well, none. I just told you he's been assigned as an oiler."

"So he hasn't had any practice or experience in radar maintenance since he joined your outfit?"

". . . No, I guess not."

Here, then, was a maintenance man who had spent several months learning a rather complex skill; but for six months he had had no opportunity to practice that skill. No wonder his test performance was poor. No wonder there was a difference between what he could do and what he was expected to be able to do.

The battery commander also saw the point. Instead of chastising the maintenance man, he assigned him immediately to maintenance duty (under the watchful eye of a more experienced man).

This was an instance in which:

• There was a genuine performance discrepancy.
• It was important.
• It was due to a skill deficiency.
• The skill was once there, but had been forgotten.

It was a classic case of a skill withering away for lack of exercise. Other examples are not hard to find.

The manager of an engineering group found himself involved with one of those "panic" projects that somehow keep imposing themselves on our routines. His staff had only 36 hours in which to complete preparation of a rather complex proposal, and they were busy making calculations, preparing graphs, and editing copy. The manager had been an engineer once himself, so he took out his slide rule, rolled up his sleeves, and joined his staff at work.

Alas, he made error after error. He just couldn't seem to get things right the first time. And it didn't take him long to see the problem. Though he kept his trusty slide rule in the top drawer of his desk, lack of practice led to some forgetting. Some of his slick slip-stick skill had silently slipped away (more rusty than trusty?).

Getting a little personal now . . .

RFM: Peter, didn't you used to live in San Francisco?

PP: Yes.

RFM: Then how come you get lost when you drive there?

PP: Come on, now. I don't *always* get lost. Just most of the time.

RFM: Why?

PP: Well, it all seems so familiar that I don't bother with maps—and then I find I've forgotten some of the streets. I don't get much practice any more. Haven't *you* ever forgotten anything from lack of practice?

RFM: Not very much. Only most of what I learned in school.

PP: Wastrel!

RFM: Wait a minute! I remember from seventh grade biology that the esophagus has a pyloric valve on the end of it.

PP: How nice. What else do you remember?

RFM: Ah-h . . . mmm . . . wel-l-l-l . . .

PP: Didn't you used to be good at math?

RFM: Not actually good, but I used to know how to solve calculus problems and how to do things like analysis of variance. But I couldn't do them today. Never needed them.

PP: But you could relearn them, don't you think?

RFM: Sure I could.

PP: Exactly the point. You used to be able to do things you can't do now, but you could relearn them in less time than it took first time around.

In none of these cases would we propose the expensive route of formal courses of instruction. If we want to sustain these once-known skills at an acceptable level, then the need is probably for a "skill maintenance program" of the kind described in the next chapter.

For now, we will simply call your attention to the importance of those questions that help you decide whether a skill deficiency is due to some form of forgetting or to the fact that it never existed. If it never existed, there's a good chance that training will be indicated. But if it once existed and now is lost, strayed, or stolen, training from scratch would be a more expensive remedy than you need.

Whether you answer "yes" or "no" to "Could they do it in the past?" (Did each person once know how to perform as desired?), you still can't tell what the problem is. More questions are needed. We'll make a start on them in the next chapter.

What to Do

Determine whether the skill once existed.

How to Do It

Ask these questions:

- *Did the person once know how to perform as desired?*
- *Has the person forgotten how to do what I want done?*

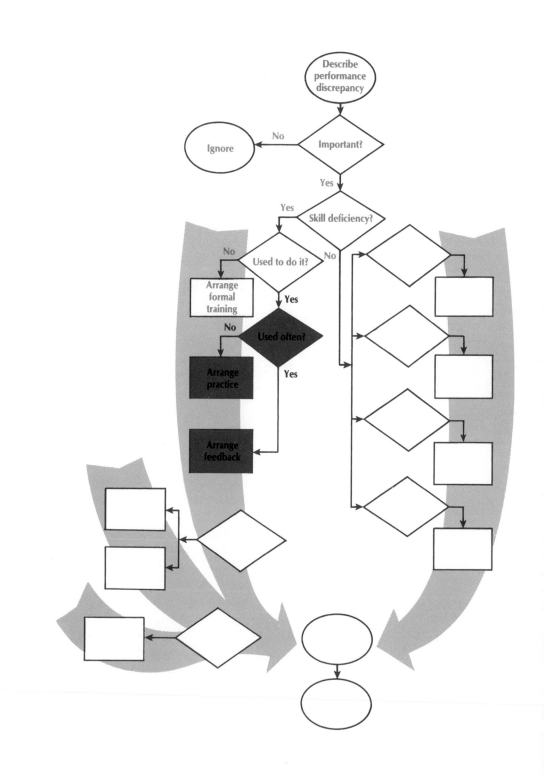

5 | Is the Skill Used Often?

■ **WHERE WE ARE**

An important performance discrepancy exists, and it is a genuine skill deficiency. At one time the person was able to perform as desired.

When a skill fades or disappears, an appropriate remedy to consider is a skill maintenance program. Skill maintenance programs come in two major forms. One kind, as was the case with the radar man discussed in the preceding chapter, is meant to help someone "stay in practice." It is a systematic honing of an important skill or state of knowledge that has to be used only occasionally.

The police departments of the country recognized long ago that though police officers rarely use their guns, they must be accurate shots when the need arises. To keep their accuracy within acceptable limits, officers are required to practice regularly on a pistol range—a performance maintenance program.

The concert pianist practices and practices between concerts, not only to increase his or her skill, but to maintain it. Pianists know that the fine edge of an existing skill can deteriorate rather quickly.

Both of these examples are cases in which performance (and peak performance, at that) is required only occasionally or infrequently. In these cases, periodic practice is the useful remedy. The more critical the skill, the more important that this practice be provided.

But there is another type of situation in which the second kind of skill maintenance program is needed—practice with feedback. This is the case where:

- A skill deficiency exists.
- The person used to be able to perform the skill well.
- *The skill is in constant use.*

These are situations in which, paradoxically, performance deteriorates *despite* constant practice. And this is a totally different problem from situations where performance withered away because of lack of practice.

But isn't it true that "practice makes perfect"?

Unfortunately, that ragged old adage is misleading. Practice makes perfect *only* when you have information about how well you are practicing. In fact, if you have no way of knowing how well you are doing, practice may serve merely to entrench poor or imperfect actions. Your marksmanship with a gun will not be improved if you merely shoot at the moon. Your pronunciation of a foreign language will not improve unless you can hear the difference between your way of speaking and a native's way of speaking. Practice without feedback is of little value.

The Case of the Slipping Solderers

In an electronics assembly plant, high precision was demanded of women soldering components together. On joining the company, they were taught to solder, and they were not allowed on the production line until they could consistently make acceptable solder joints. On the job, it was found that the quality of soldered joints tended to fall off after a few weeks, even though the women made hundreds of joints each day. Why?

It was hard to get feedback about the quality of each soldered joint as it was made. You couldn't necessarily tell just by looking. It wasn't practical to make immediate mechanical and electrical tests of each connection. Faulty work in a subassembly may not have been discovered until many joints had been made by many operators. Tracking down the faulty connection and the operator concerned was possible, but costly.

Once again, a performance maintenance program was useful. This time, though, practice was not the primary function. Here it *maintained* skill level by providing the operator with periodic feedback about the quality of her work. All operators were required to renew their certificate of competence every six months. If they checked out, fine; if not, they were given some brief brush-up training. This, it was found, was enough to keep them up to snuff.

The Case of the Diminishing Driver

A friend recently complained, "That's the *third* traffic ticket I've had in a month. I've been driving for ten years and never had a citation—and all of a sudden they start picking on me!"

Hmmm. Wasn't it more likely that his driving skill had slipped somewhat, even though he got plenty of practice? After all, you don't get feedback for every infraction, for every display of poor or dangerous car handling. There is no one there to inform you each time you forget a turn signal, or cut another driver short, or make a turn from the wrong lane, or follow another car too closely. When people *do* get feedback in the form of a traffic citation, they seldom recognize this as an indication of slipshod driving; instead, there is the tendency to point that ever-ready finger—in someone else's direction. (If fingers were as lethal as 45's, we'd *all* be dead by now.)

The Case of the Perpetual Performers

"But I interview more than a dozen people a day," grumped the manager, "and now you tell me I don't do it right? I get more practice at interviewing than anyone in the plant."

She was right. She interviewed more people than anyone else around. And yet . . . and yet there was something about her performance that rubbed people the wrong way. Here was still another instance in which the performance was less than adequate, even though the skill was exercised frequently.

What was happening? No feedback. She never found out that she was irritating some of her interviewees. The people interviewed certainly wouldn't tell her, and those who heard them grumble only commented among themselves. So why should this manager behave differently when there was no feedback to suggest why and how?

Isn't this something we all experience in everyday living? We spend a lot of time interacting with others, and hence get a lot of practice at it. Yet how often does someone take us aside and offer real honest-to-goodness feedback that would help us do it better? Practically never, right?

Any time performance is something other than what is desired, and there is reason to believe that the desired perform-ance could be within the person's capabilities, check to see whether he or she is receiving regular information about the quality of the performance.

So, if a frequently used skill slips, look for lack of feedback as the probable cause. If an infrequently used skill slips, look for lack of practice as a probable cause. Perhaps it would help to see the situation graphically.

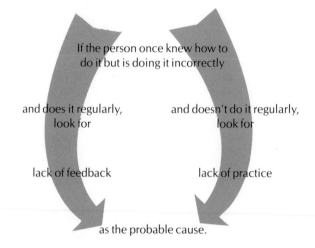

If the person once knew how to
do it but is doing it incorrectly

and does it regularly,   and doesn't do it regularly,
look for   look for

lack of feedback   lack of practice

as the probable cause.

As with other causes of performance deficiencies, an additional remedy is to change or simplify the job, to modify the performance that is required or expected. As an example, the captain of a jetliner, no matter how grizzled and wise he may be, must use a checklist to ensure that he covers everything in his preflight inspection. There's nothing unprofessional about using such an aid; in fact, the unprofessional person is the one who tries to get away without using the checklist. Thus, instead of trying to upgrade someone's performance, even if that performance once existed, you can sometimes solve the problem by providing help. Further examples will be offered in Chapter 6.

What to Do

Determine whether the lost or deteriorated skill is used frequently or infrequently.

- If the skill is used frequently *but has deteriorated despite regular use, maintain the level of performance by providing periodic feedback.*
- If the skill is used infrequently, *maintain the level of performance by providing a regular schedule of practice.*

How to Do It

Ask these questions:

- *How often is the skill or performance used?*
- *Is there regular feedback on performance?*
- *Exactly how does the person find out how well he or she is doing?*

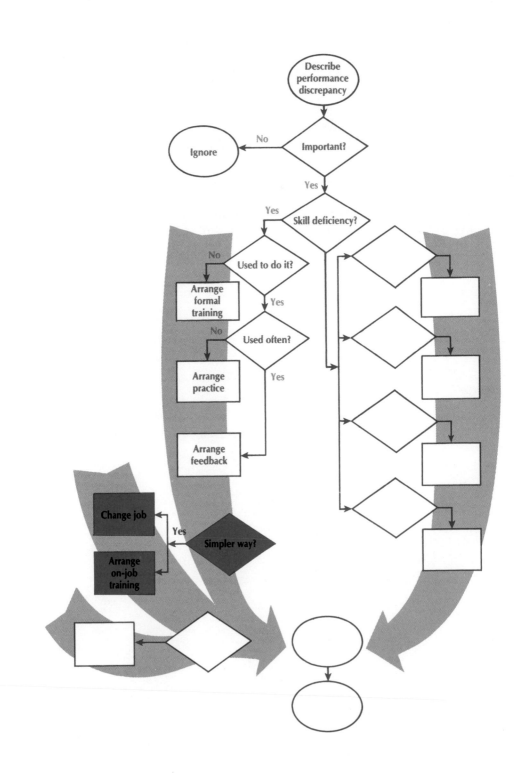

6 Is There a Simpler Solution?

■ WHERE WE ARE

An important performance discrepancy exists. It's a genuine skill deficiency, something the person cannot do. Depending upon other conditions, three tentative solutions have been identified: (1) If the skill was familiar but is now used only rarely, consider systematic practice. (2) If the skill is familiar and is in regular use, consider providing more feedback. (3) If the skill is lacking, consider formal training.

We are still only exploring possibilities. We have three tentative solutions, but there are two more questions to ask about each situation before the problem can be clearly defined: (1) Is there a simpler way? (2) Does the individual have the potential to benefit from this solution?

In answer to the first question, there's one universal alternative that may be simpler and less expensive than any solution so far proposed. It's changing the job—changing the skill requirements to meet the skills available. Examples of changing the job:

- If instead of requiring someone to remember a sequence of steps, you provide a checklist to which the person can refer any time he or she wants to know what to do next, you have changed the job. You have simplified it, and presumably it can now be handled by someone with lesser capabilities.
- If you provide machinery for lifting heavy loads, so that an individual no longer has to lift manually, you have changed the job. You have done away with the need for certain physical characteristics. On the other hand, you may have added a need for the ability to master the use of the machinery.

We hope that this sounds obvious. In practice, it may be less obvious. Somehow, tasks themselves, the standards, or the means of performing can become hallowed by precedent ("That's the way it's always been done"), or by apparent acceptance in high places ("That's how the boss wants it done"), or through many other appeals to authenticity that make the present desired performance the one and only way.

Examples are all around us of ways in which a task has been simplified through the use of instructions, aids, or checklists, eliminating the need for formal instruction. Any number of household appliances, for example, require that you learn something before they can be used properly. But their manufacturers don't provide a course; they provide a leaflet or booklet. And a look at the instructions is generally enough to do the trick.

A rather similar solution works well when the knowledge needed to carry out an infrequent task is simple to acquire. Rather than teach a course and try to store information in the head of every potential user, you put instructions where they can be seen readily. For example, if you have forgotten how to use a fire extinguisher, instructions carried on the device will refresh your memory in a second or two. Bought a new car? Read the manual and you will be ready to go.

In the best of all possible worlds, every household might have available at all times a person able to render first aid for all conceivable cases of poisoning. But most of us take care of that problem adequately by fastening a list of poison antidotes to the door of the broom closet. The specifics of what to do in each particular situation are, in fact, better stored on the closet door than in someone's head. A wait of a minute or two might be less dangerous than giving the victim the wrong antidote.

The situation is similar for the "critical" skill known as fire drill. You have people practice fire drill procedures so they will be able to get out of a burning building by the quickest and safest route. You may institute emergency procedures, such as telephoning for help. But you also display the emergency telephone number by the phones, and attach instructions for using the fire extinguishers to individual extinguishers.

You can just imagine the chaos if every person who prepared airline tickets had to *remember* all the information there is to know about fares, flight times, destinations, flight numbers, days the flights are operative, and a gaggle of other details. Even if such were possible, the problem would be multiplied every time there was a *change* in ticket prices and schedules. With the information stored in a computer instead of stuffed into someone's head, it is easily and accurately available and easy to change.

The more complex the job, or the more critical it is that it be performed correctly, the stronger the argument for introducing a performance aid rather than expecting people to be "fully trained." If you have a task that is performed infrequently, and which is also both complex and critical, you have every reason to find ways of reducing the need for human skills such as recalling and making judgments.

Industry has found that errors can be eliminated by labeling the controls of equipment. Color coding can also reduce errors and the need for training. Color-coded pathways on warehouse floors tell forklift operators where to travel and where to store what; color-coded gas tanks tell the anesthesiologist their content; gas pumps at the service station are color-coded for easier recognition; price tags in clothing stores are often color-coded according to size; and sets of books are often color-coded by a publisher for easier identification.

Consider the case of the meter readers. Women at the end of a production line making electronic products recorded the electrical characteristics of each product so that an accept/reject decision could be made. To do so, they took about six readings from as many meters, and wrote down the numbers on a card.

In an ordinary day, each woman made hundreds of readings; and many of them had had months, even years, of experience. But when their meter-reading accuracy was measured one day, it was found to be only 40 percent! Interestingly, a group of women with no special training in reading meters performed at the same level.

How could this be? If experience is the best teacher, why didn't the meter readers get better rather than worse?

The answer proved to be that they never found out whether their readings were accurate. In time, their accuracy diminished.

Aha! Isn't the answer obvious? Where there is no feedback for performance, the thing to do is to arrange for feedback. Sometimes, though, that's easier said than done, as in this case. So what's the alternative? Nearly always, one possibility is to change the job in order to eliminate the performance for which it is difficult to arrange feedback. Here, the company provided an aid to performance by installing meters that show their readings directly in numerals, rather than by the movement of a pointer along a scale.

If you've reached this point via the argument that leads to "consider formal training," you have special reason to be wary, since formal training is probably the most expensive solution of all. It pays to take an extra-hard second look when your instinctive response is "We need another course."

A few years ago, the powers-that-be asked the instructional technology department of a British military group to determine if some programmed instruction would be useful in a five-day course in the maintenance of teletypewriter equipment. The course had been continually refined throughout its existence, but the management wanted to make it even better.

The instructional technologists knew their trade, however, and didn't fall into the trap of just looking at the existing curriculum to see what pieces of it might be programmed. Instead, they performed a task analysis to see what the repair people did when performing their job. They started from the beginning in order to find out whether there was a discrepancy between what students *entering* the course could do and what they were required to do on the job. They wanted to know if that discrepancy was a genuine skill deficiency.

It was, and so they asked questions to determine how best to eliminate the discrepancy. As a result, not only did they *not* prepare any programmed instruction for the existing course, but the existing course was, as they say in England, disestablished. Cancelled.

Why? Because they found that what trainees needed to learn could easily be picked up on the job with observation and informal instruction and practice. Formal instruction was a more elaborate solution than needed—like using an elephant to crack peanuts or a computer to add the grocery bill. Had the analysis been conducted before the course was set up in the first place, it is doubtful that such an extensive effort would have been proposed to stuff into the students' heads that which was either not needed or already there.

The Case of the Careless Copiers

Recently we ran into an interesting example at a large company that makes copying machines, among other things. People in the marketing department had noted that an unusually large percentage of customers using one model of copier were having difficulty operating the machine.

"They just don't know how to insert the toner bottle." (That's a plastic bottle filled with the black powder that makes the printed image.) "All they have to do is slide it along IN the track, but they slide it ON TOP of the track instead. Then there's a mess, and the customer calls the maintenance people. It's damned expensive."

As you might expect, the first solution proposed was to train the customers. Analysis showed, however, that the performance discrepancy was a "sort-of" skill deficiency; the operators could sort-of do it if they really had to, but they found it hard to do it correctly without paying a great deal of attention. Further analysis revealed that the task could be simplified by painting a stripe on the machine where the toner bottle was to be inserted, and a similar stripe on the bottles themselves. The instruction could then be simply, "Line up the stripes when inserting bottle." The cost of this proposed solution was about $15,000. Compared to what it might have cost to train customers to perform the task more accurately without the performance aid, it was a good solution, indeed.

In summary, even when a genuine skill deficiency exists, any solution to the problem should be weighed against the possibility of changing the job—particularly through providing some kind of job aids (checklists, instruction sheets, signs, labels, color coding, and the like). If training seems to be the only remedy, on-the-job training may be easier and cheaper, and just as good as the formal variety. As one of the sages of the business, Thomas Gilbert, puts it, "Show-how is cheaper than know-how."

What to Do

Determine if there is a solution simpler than performance maintenance or formal training.

How to Do It

Ask these questions:

- *Can I change the job by providing some kind of job aid?*
- *Can I store the needed information some way (in written instructions, checklists) other than in someone's head?*
- *Can I show rather than train?*
- *Would informal (such as on-the-job) training be sufficient?*

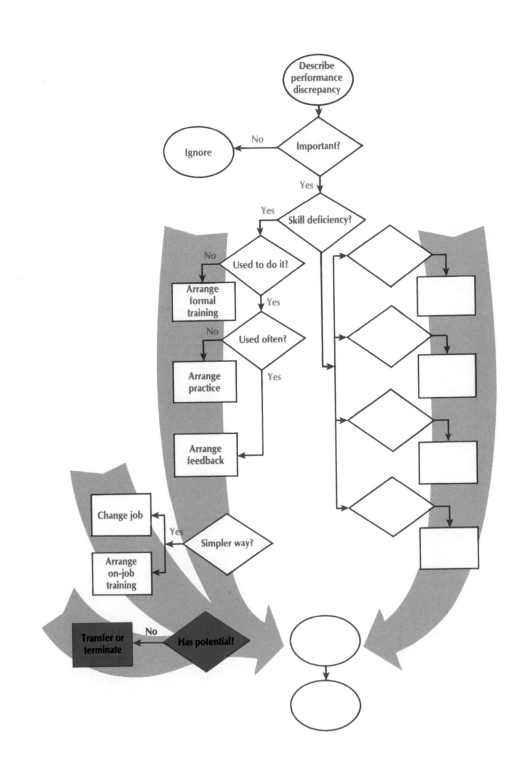

7 | Do They Have What It Takes?

An important performance discrepancy has been identified as a genuine skill deficiency. Depending upon conditions, we have identified one of the following as a possible solution: (1) provide feedback to keep a frequently used skill up to standard, *or* (2) provide periodic practice to sustain an infrequently used skill, *or* (3) provide formal training, *or* (4) provide some simpler type of training, *or* (5) change the requirements of the job.

All five of our possible ways of tackling different causes of genuine deficiencies in performance must still be considered tentative. One more dimension must be added to our statement of the problem by asking this question: Do nonperformers have the potential to benefit from this change?

You can make all the changes you like; but if an individual doesn't have what it takes, either mentally or physically, to do the job, the changes are a waste of time.

Any time someone cannot handle an existing job, you're stuck, inevitably, with the two universal alternatives to all of the solutions proposed in this book: change the job or change the person. The first alternative was discussed in the previous chapter. The second is the subject of this chapter.

"Changing the person" means, of course, to substitute another individual for the apparent nonperformer. Sometimes it's quite plain that this is inevitable, as when physical limitations prevent performance. The decision to transfer or fire, however, is not always as straightforward as it may seem when your patience is running out. In fact, to look at a problem with anger or impatience is to look at it through a distorting lens.

On a production line making very tiny products, for example, a foreman complained that one woman made considerably more mistakes than anyone else. Like the others, she peered through a binocular microscope to see the tiny parts and to assist with their assembly. She assembled the same product as the others, and under the same conditions. But she was considerably "clumsier" than the others. The foreman wanted to get rid of her—that was his solution.

This case came to the attention of the training department, and its members looked around and asked questions. They quickly discovered that this worker was not looking through the microscope with *both* eyes as she should have been. She looked with only one eye at a time. She didn't know that looking with both eyes at the same time made any difference when the instrument was properly adjusted. But without the depth perception that comes with using both eyes simultaneously, she could not see well enough to assemble accurately. Hence, she was labeled "clumsy."

After only two or three *minutes* of instruction in the proper use of the microscope, the woman's work was the equal of all the others in the department. She wasn't clumsy, or unmotivated, or incapable of learning. She was simply prevented from doing the job well by lack of information.

The remedies of transfer and termination are used more often than they should be. They are the crude hatchets of those unsophisticated in their knowledge of the limits of human performance, a sign of failure to locate less traumatic remedies. They should be considered a last resort rather than a first.

The issue of "potential to perform" should be approached in two stages: Could the person learn the job? Does he or she have what it takes to do the job?

If people can learn a job they can do it, can't they? Not necessarily. It sounds contradictory, but some people become underperformers because they are overqualified for the job.

Some companies court trouble without realizing it by following a policy of overhiring. "We always hire the best people available," they boast; and then they go on to set people to work at jobs that are beneath their abilities. College graduates are put to work as glorified typists, or given simple tasks on a production line; engineers find themselves working in the drafting department. Managers who succumb to this temptation are bewildered when dissatisfaction appears in its many guises—low morale, absenteeism, edginess, uncooperativeness, and so on.

In a company we know, inspectors tested some complex electronic devices at the end of assembly. They did so by connecting the devices to their test equipment and checking readings on dials. The day shift inspector was an older woman who had little idea of *why* she was doing these things. She did what she was trained to do and hooked up the devices and recorded the readings. If the readings deviated from those specified, she rejected the device.

The night shift inspection, on the other hand, was handled by a young woman who was a doctoral candidate in the arts at a nearby university. She found an intellectual challenge in any task. To counteract her boredom with the job routine, she worked hard at finding out all she could about the how and why of the manufacture of the devices. Eventually, she was able to hold an intelligent conversation about the devices with engineers. Because of her increased knowledge, she began to *interpret* the readings on her test equipment. She no longer adhered to the strict accept/reject instructions of her training. As a result, she began to accept devices that should not have been accepted and to send others back for expensive reworking when they should have been accepted.

It's always a temptation to put the "best" available person into a job. But when that person is much overqualified, the rewards can be short-lived. A more realistic matching of skills with jobs will avoid the boredom and lack of challenge that lead to performance discrepancies after the first rush of enthusiasm.

The problem of overqualification can arise at home, too. Take the case of the teenager assigned to the carrying-out-the-garbage detail. The young are notoriously (and perhaps rightly) impatient of activities they consider boring. So the teenager fights carrying out the garbage.

"I'm his father/mother," you say. "Why should I get stuck with this chore when I have this son/daughter sitting around? Isn't it boring for me, too?" Yes, of course. But emotional issues aside, the teenager is bored and wants to be involved in something more exciting. Garbage-carrying loses out when it competes with doing, or even dreaming about, most other activities. The rewards of garbage-carrying have to be competitive with those real or imagined delights—a good trick. The least this tells you is that those who work at tasks for which they are overqualified need some extrinsic reward to take the place of "satisfaction in the job." (More on that later.)

Following the lead discussed in the previous chapter, you may wonder whether the task can be simplified or made more interesting. Why is there so much garbage? Could the amount be reduced? (Eat your spinach!) If it could, that might make for fewer trips to the can. How about installing a disposal? Or a trash masher? That might reduce the number of trips still further.

How about making the task more interesting? One father we know claims he hasn't had any trouble at all getting the kids to mow the lawn—since he bought a motorized lawn mower that they can sit on and drive!

Meanwhile, back to the point of this chapter. "Do they have the potential?" refers only in part to intellectual capacity, as mentioned earlier. *Appropriateness* for the task or job is another facet to consider. A person may have all the mental and physical qualities needed to do the job, and still be wrong for it.

"I suppose I could learn to fill out that crummy tax form, but I'll hate it."

"Sure I can do the job, but I just don't like to work in cold weather. You just might as well not send me there in the first place."

"I can do the job OK, but not with that music blaring all day long."

"No, I don't *want* to do that job, no matter how good I might get at it."

In each case the person is wrong for the job, whatever it may be. There's a lack of inclination. When people so plainly announce themselves to be square pegs, they lack the potential for sustained performance.

In summary, it is useful to determine whether someone has the capacity to do the job required, and whether he or she would "fit" the job mentally and motivationally even if the performance in question were brought up to standard. If the answer to both questions is "yes," go ahead with your solution.

What to Do

Determine whether the person has the potential to perform as desired.

How to Do It

Ask these questions:

- *Could the person learn the job (is the individual trainable)?*

- *Does this person have the physical and mental potential to perform as desired?*

- *Is this person overqualified for the job?*

PART

III

It Is Not a Skill Deficiency.

They Could Do It if They Wanted To.

Could nonperformers perform if they had to? This pivotal question was asked immediately after we determined that we were looking at an important performance discrepancy (Chapter 3). To this point, we've looked at several solutions that apply when the answer is plainly "No. Even if their lives depended on it, they couldn't do it." Now we're going back to the question to see what happens when the answer is something other than that unequivocal "no."

When you know or suspect that a person could perform if he or she really had to, it's probably plain that something other than instruction is needed. In general, the remedy is that of *performance management*. Rather than modify the person's skill or knowledge (since it's likely that the ability already exists), you will have to modify the conditions associated with the performance, or the consequence or result of that performance. Rather than change what the person *can* do, change something about the world in which he or she does it so that doing it will be more attractive, or less repulsive, or less difficult.

You will get clues that a problem is mainly one of performance management, rather than performance teaching, from statements such as:

"She just isn't motivated."
"He just doesn't *want* to do it."
"She simply doesn't *care.*"
"He's too lazy to do it."
"She doesn't have the right attitude."
"He oughta wanna do it."
"I'm too busy to do it."
"I'm not allowed to do it."
"That isn't my job."
"They'll fire me if I do it."
"They'll laugh at me if I do it."

These statements hint that the person probably *could* perform as desired, but isn't. They suggest that the skill in question is already within the repertoire of the person being described, but that it is not being used. They are the clues that indicate a situation that might be described as "plenty of skill but not enough will." You can be pretty sure that to influence the individual to perform as desired, you must change the environment around the performance in some way rather than try to teach more skills.

There are four general causes of such nonperformance:

1. It is punishing to perform as desired.
2. It is rewarding to perform other than as desired.
3. It simply doesn't matter whether performance is as desired.
4. There are obstacles to performing as desired.

We will consider what each of these causes looks like in real life, and offer key questions for spotting them. We'll also suggest remedies.

Once again, we emphasize that no sequence of priority or importance is implied by the order in which we have listed the causes or the position in which we have placed them in the flow diagram. Consider them in any order you prefer. We urge only that you consider all of them before deciding that your analysis is complete. It will usually pay you to go over them more than once, since each answer you get may change your perception of the problem.

We now return to the point in our flow diagram where we determined whether the discrepancy in performance was due to a skill deficiency. This time we will look at the implications of "No. This is *not* a case of skill deficiency."

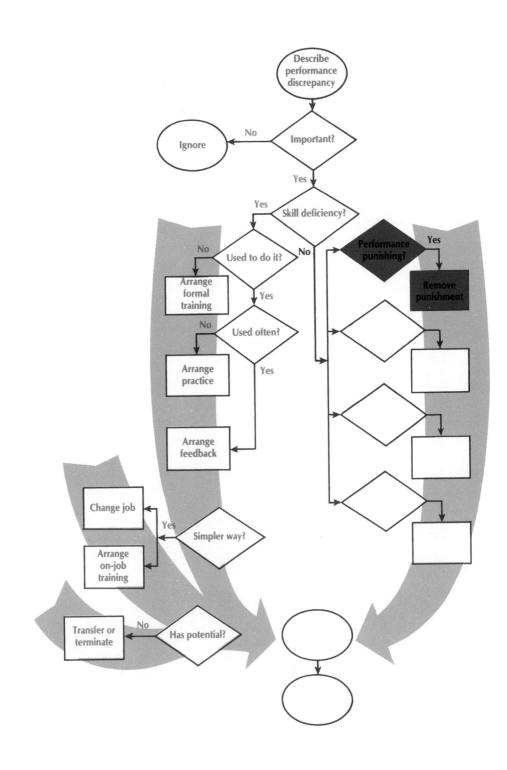

8 | Is Desired Performance Punishing?

▪ WHERE WE ARE

An important discrepancy is known or suspected *not* to be due to a skill deficiency. (That is, the person could perform if he or she had to or wanted to.)

The most common reason people don't do as they are expected to do is simply that the desired "doing" is punishing. And when desired performance leads to undesirable results, people have a way of finding other ways to go. Here are several examples.

A college music student had the chance to play with his city's symphony orchestra. For a student who had not yet completed his training, this was a rare opportunity. Since he needed both the money and the experience, he asked his music teacher if something could be worked out.

"I think so," replied the teacher. "There is no reason why you shouldn't take the job, provided you make up the school work you miss on the days you are absent."

So, the student threw himself into both tasks. He did well with the symphony and earned "A's" and "B's" on all his make-up work. But when grading time arrived, he found himself with a "C" for the course. Astonished, he asked his teacher why he was given only a "C" after receiving "A's" and "B's" for all his work.

She replied: "Well, you're getting entirely too much experience and not enough learning."

If you were the student, how would you feel in such a situation? No matter how you slice it, this is a situation in which desirable activity is followed by an unpleasant consequence (punishment). If, as a result of this dampening, the student were to perform his school work with less enthusiasm, one can imagine the teacher telling her colleagues, "You know, we've got to teach him to have the right attitude about his studies. He oughta wanna have more interest."

Recently one of us was assigned the task of "fixing the doctors' attitudes" at a large hospital. Seems that the hospital had just installed a computer, and doctors were now expected to *type* their medical orders into a terminal twice a day, instead of scribbling them unintelligibly on a pad.

"But they're not doing that," explained management. "Instead, they're grumbling about it, doing it wrong, or trying to get the nurses to do it for them." When asked, "Why should the doctors do it willingly?" management replied, "Because it's good for the hospital and patient. The labs get the medication orders a lot faster, inventory can be kept up more easily, and the billing is more accurate."

In other words, lots of good consequences for the hospital, but what about the doctors? Desired performance was punishing—in spades.

After two days of on-site observation, here is what was found. The terminals were placed in the nursing stations—very busy, public, and crowded places. As a result, there was no place to put a piece of paper down to the left or right of a terminal; and as each terminal top was "modern-designed" to slope downward, any paper placed there would slither to the floor. Now, doctors tend not to be a typing population. Some type competently, but most don't; and many think of typing as somewhat demeaning "clerk's work." The result was that most doctors would sit at terminals, notes in one hand, with the "proctological" finger of the other hand laboriously "hunting 'n' pecking" away at their medical orders.

The nurses, who had banded together to agree not to take over this chore, would tend to stand in the background and snicker. After all, they typed on the terminals regularly and were pretty good at it.

There's more. The terminals were mounted on tables 30 inches high. That's no problem for you with your perfect vision, but those of us who wear bifocals find ourselves sitting at terminals with our heads tilted back and our necks getting stiff. The same thing happened to many doctors. Had you observed them you would have noticed that after a short while of sitting with heads bent back, some would (unconsciously, it seemed) slide out of their seats, push the chairs to the tables, and then look *down* at the screens. This was far more comfortable for the necks and eyes, but it led to another source of punishment. When they picked up light pens to touch the screens and thus enter their orders into the computer, they sometimes hit the "Erase" spot rather than the "Enter" spot and erased all of their hard work. You see, the programmer had put the "Enter" code on the screen right next to the "Erase" code. When the doctors were looking *down* at a screen they might hit the wrong spot because of parallax (the bending of light by the thickness of the glass screen, much as water bends light and makes a partially submerged stick look bent).

Adding it all up, desired performance (typing orders into a terminal) was mildly painful, humiliating, and exasperating. Should anyone be surprised that there was some grumbling?

The solution was simple. Two terminals were installed on low tables in the doctors' office complex. There, each doctor could enter medical orders at his or her convenience, in private and in relative comfort.

Examples of instances in which desired performance is punished are everywhere. Sometimes the source(s) of punishment are highly visible, as in the example above, and sometimes they are more subtle.

"Trainees just won't read the material they are assigned before coming to the course," instructors often complain.

But why should they? What happens if they *do*? Well, the instructor goes over the material anyhow, and thus creates a boring time for those who did as expected.

What happens to the trainees if they *don't* do as requested? Nothing. So desired performance is often punishing, and undesired performance is largely ignored. Is it any wonder people don't do the reading assignments?

In one welfare office the supervisors complained that social workers weren't closing as many cases as they should.

"Not everyone stays on welfare for generations," a supervisor explained, "and social workers should be helping people to establish objectives and accomplish them, and thus close cases."

But consider the consequences to the social workers. If they *closed* cases, they had, in their own words, "to open other cases. And that takes a lot of legwork until each case settles down." By "settle down" they meant that in time, cases usually become routine and can be handled with periodic phone calls or visits.

What happened to them if they *didn't* close cases? The supervisors complained . . . among themselves. Worse, the social workers complained among *them*selves that the supervisors preferred that they produce fat reports with lots of psychiatric language, rather than good records for closing cases.

An insurance company had a policy of trying to recruit upper-level managers from the ranks of its field agencies. But the agency managers resisted the promotions. One of them described the situation this way:

"They tell me it would be good for the company if I accepted the promotion and moved to corporate headquarters back East. But why would I want to do that? The raise doesn't mean that much. Besides, I'm my own boss here. I do the hiring and firing, I set the working hours. I know everybody in town; I belong to the club and play golf with my friends. Why should I give up all this just to sit in a concrete blockhouse back East?"

From this agency manager's point of view, the performance desired by head-office management (accepting the promotion) would definitely make his world dimmer. And if a consequence makes someone's world dimmer, less pleasant, or less interesting, you can consider that a punishing consequence. In this example not only was desired performance punishing, but *non*performance (staying on as agency manager) was highly rewarding. In situations such as these, it is little short of folly to expect that "inspirational lectures" or exhortation will do much good.

Punishment for desired or superior performance is so common that one may overlook it in an area where it frequently occurs—the family. Yet it's plain to see in what we call the "anti-intellectual family." Sons or daughters who aspire to rise above the intellectual level of their relatives, or who set their sights on occupations different from those pursued by relatives, or who raise their conversations above the level of the family "norm," are not applauded, or revered, or urged to greater heights; but instead are insulted and stung with ridicule so that they lose their motivation to escape their mental ghettos.

There are many more cases around the home where desired performance is withheld because of its unfavorable consequence. Parents complain, "I don't know what they teach 'em in school these days, but our kids don't come to us with their questions and problems like they used to." Observe these same parents in interaction with their children, however, and it quickly becomes apparent that the parents are the cause of the problem.

> *Kid:* Hey, Mom 'n' Dad! Look what I made in school today!
>
> *Parent:* Wipe your mouth!

Little wonder the kids behave as they do. The parents, all unintentionally, perhaps, have engineered it that way. And usually they couldn't have done a better job if they had been trying.

These examples are designed to remind you of a simple truth about human behavior:

People learn to avoid the things they are hit with!

It doesn't matter whether they are hit with a club, an insult, humiliation, repeated failure, frustration, or boredom. If people feel they will be punished, or even that there is a risk of being punished when they perform as you desire, they will avoid doing it your way whenever they can. People don't often do things that will lead to their world being dimmer than it is.

A classic example from industry is the comparative emphasis on safety and production. Management says, "Safety is our top priority. Right after it comes productivity."

But what does a supervisor's reputation depend upon? Production. You'll rarely hear, "Great supervisor. Tremendous safety record. This is the person we'll promote."

Safety managers complain that as long as nothing goes wrong—as long as people "get away with it"—nobody cares about safety.

Production is seen as the result that counts. And despite the lip service, safety takes a second (or third, or fourth) seat in the perception of those affected.

And so, when people aren't performing as desired, and you know that they *could* do so, one thing to explore is whether it isn't unnecessarily punishing to perform that way. Is there an undesirable consequence (result) for doing it your way? Do they see desired performance as being geared to penalties? If so, you have probably located a strong reason why you aren't getting the results you would like.

We must emphasize, however, that it is not *your* view of the outcome that is important here. You must try to see the situation through the eyes of the people whose performances you would change and ask yourself, "What is the result to *them* for doing as I desire? How might *they* see the consequences of doing it?" What may be favorable consequences to *you* could be *un*favorable to *them*.

On occasion, this can be subtle. Sometimes it may strike you as ridiculous. No matter. Listen to what the performers say.

The employer complains, "I don't see why he won't work overtime—he makes good money on it." But the employee says, "What's the good of overtime. Anything you earn, they take away in taxes."

The parent says, "I don't see why she won't take math. It will get her a better job when she's grown." But the student says, "Math is for those types who want to follow the establishment road. I'm interested in people. Besides, the math teacher is the least liked guy in the whole school."

Or consider the case of the "rate buster" in school or industry—the one who turns out more work than anyone else. Do colleagues revere this person for his or her skill or industriousness? It's more likely that the group's attitude will be perceived as punishment for performance, and the person will slow down to the level of the group . . . or be pushed out of it.

Did you ever attend a school where the consequence of knowing your subject or of showing your intelligence was ridicule from other students? Where the "in" thing was not to do homework and not to make good grades? Where diligent students were dismissed as "eggheads" and "brains," and worse?

You hear teachers and administrators complain that students don't do their homework. "These students oughta wanna do their homework. If they don't, they will be doomed to a lifetime of mediocrity." And then, because teachers and administrators fail to look at the problem from the students' viewpoint, they make new policies that only aggravate the situation.

In such a case, homework is doubly punishing for the students. They perceive it first as an onerous duty that replaces more pleasant activities. If, despite this, they do the homework, it may lead to consequences in which the lumps they take from their peers may outweigh more positive outcomes such as good grades and teacher approval. So they don't do their homework. So the school invents new punitive policies, and more threat of failure is laid on. And so the students perceive yet another reason why it's necessary to beat the system. One can't help thinking of two gladiators beating each other to death with bloodied clubs, each telling the other he oughta wanna be the first to stop. For no matter what the school does, it cannot invent a consequence aversive enough to outweigh the ridicule of peers.

A more effective way to break the miserable chain of events would be to make the consequence of studying more immediately favorable than those that now exist, so that those who study successfully will have reason to be envied rather than ridiculed. Rather than continue to argue that students "oughta wanna" *for their own good*, make desired privileges dependent upon the performance wanted. Instead of saying, "You will fail if you don't learn," make the rule say that if students learn they may have an extra free period, or they will be allowed to come and go as they please, or they will be entitled to some other thing they really find desirable.

Several years ago the clinical faculty of a dental school complained that students were putting in too little laboratory time on dentures they were making for their patients. The situation was this. Students treated their patients in the clinic.

When adjustments were needed in the fitting of dentures, the student would go to the laboratory to make adjustments and then return to the patient in the clinic to try again. The complaint of the faculty was that the students were not as painstaking as they should have been and as they *knew how to be* in getting dentures to fit. "We've got to teach them to be less careless," was the cry. "We've got to teach them to have the right attitude."

So here's another situation in which a person has the skill to perform as desired, but for some reason is *not* performing as desired. But what would the faculty "teach" the students to remedy this performance discrepancy? What would they put in a curriculum—molar appreciation? How could they "encourage the right attitude"?

When the question "What is the consequence of performing correctly?" was finally asked, the nature of the problem became obvious. The laboratory was one floor up and at the other end of the building from the clinic. Obviously, it was less punishing to cut a few corners than to run up and down every few minutes. When the lab was finally moved next to the clinic, the quality of the dentures improved miraculously— without any instruction at all—after which the faculty ceased to complain about students' attitudes toward dentures.

The hospital provides us with another example of how it is possible to design *against* the results one wants. Patients who cannot get out of bed are provided with a call button with which to summon help. Most of the time, the system works quite well. Occasionally, however, a patient will resist pressing the call button for long periods of time—even though in great distress.

Why doesn't the patient press the button when he or she is in need? What consequence of pressing the button when help is needed might cause the patient to suffer? Is it possible button-pushing can somehow be punishing?

You bet it can! It can be embarrassing or upsetting. Occasionally, the consequence of pushing the button is to summon a grouch who bursts into the room with a "What now?" or a "Not *you* again?" It takes very few such experiences for the weakened patient to find it easier to tolerate his or her distress than to press the button for help.

Industry is no less susceptible to the situation in which desired performance is more punishing than need be. For example, the flaunting of safety regulations despite "safety training" is a familiar problem. Though people often know how to recognize and report a safety hazard, they don't. Why not?

In some departments it is considered "rocking the boat" to report safety hazards (it usually implies that someone has been sloppy or irresponsible), and in some others it is considered "chicken" to use goggles or a saw guard. But regardless of the reason, the consequence of hazard reporting is punishment. A worker may be looked down on by his or her peers, and may have to bear the brunt of insults. Some individuals may even have the "rules" of the department "explained" with a fist. There are places where it simply isn't safe to report safety hazards!

Once a problem of this kind is identified as an example of "performance is punishing," it's plain that the solution is not the usual one of handing out more information. Though there may be a number of actions used as remedies, depending on the precise circumstances, each will have to be a way of reducing the undesirable results and increasing the desirable results of desired performance. Some companies provide a bonus or recognition to departments with perfect safety records, while others may tie desired privileges to an absence of accidents over an extended period of time.

For another common if less important example, take meeting-attending behavior. Time is wasted waiting for latecomers. It persists no matter how often instructions are given or exhortations are delivered. Plainly, this isn't a miniature training problem. To get at the true problem, you have to ask: "What's the consequence of performing as desired?"

What are the results of coming on time? Well, you have to sit around and wait for latecomers.

What's the result of being late? The meeting starts almost as soon as you arrive.

ann landers

Dear Ann Landers: I have never written to you before but after I read the letter signed "Lonesome" I knew my time had come.

My in-laws are also "Lonesome" —or at least that's what they tell everybody.

We hear from many people that they complain constantly about how we ignore them and how hurt they are. It burns me up.

Last Sunday my husband and I and the kids went to see them and it was the same old story.

Grandma and Grandpa talked about nothing but how sick they are, how much they suffer (she with backaches and he with rheumatism in his legs). It is a real contest to see who is in worse shape.

Then they tell us for the 50th time about how bad their operations were. (Hers two years ago for a tumor, his five years ago for a hernia.)

They are so self-centered it is awful. Never a question about the children or my husband's job or my interests.

All they want to do is talk about themselves and their sicknesses.

Also, whenever we go to see them they greet us with, "We didn't think you were coming."

I wonder how many other "Lonesome" parents there are around? If so, maybe there's a good reason their children don't visit them more often. — Cause And Effect

Dear Cause: There are plenty around, and I hear from dozens of them. Your signature was most appropriate.

Whenever you get an "effect" like the one described in your letter there's got to be a "cause." Thanks for writing.

Reprinted by permission: Ann Landers, Field Newspaper Syndicate

Thus, punctuality is punished and tardiness is rewarded. And that's precisely the opposite of what is intended.

Another interesting problem of this sort came to our attention not long ago. A bank decided, "We've got to teach our branch managers to be a little less conservative about making loans." The remainder of the conversation with management went like this:

"Do these branch managers know how to be riskier about making loans?"

"Yes. They merely have to accept those loan applications closest to the top of the reject pile."

"Do they know you want them to be less conservative?"

"Oh, yes. We have been sending them corporate memos for the past six months, but it doesn't seem to do much good."

"What happens to the branch managers who take a conservative stance?"

"All their loans are paid back and they are looked at favorably by their superiors."

"What happens if they take the riskier stance, as desired?"

"Well, if some of their loans default, their superiors rate their performances down."

Or consider this common situation:

Manager: That's right, boss. It wasn't easy, but I managed to get my division $50,000 under budget this year.

Boss: (Beaming.) That's great! *Now* I can reduce your budget by that amount for next year.

Coming in under budget is very rewarding for the boss, but a cut in next year's budget is anything but rewarding for the manager.

It is not at all uncommon to find conflicting consequences. An example that comes to mind occurs in banks where tellers are exhorted to sell the extra services of the bank, such as special accounts and rentals of safe-deposit boxes. At the same time, tellers are expected to keep the lines of waiting customers short. Since service-selling take time, it tends to keep the lines longer. As long lines are more visible and their consequences more immediate than the selling or nonselling of services, service-selling tends to get the short end of the pickle.

So whenever you run into situations that are not skill deficiencies, look for consequences *to the performer* that somehow diminish that performer's world (that is, consequences that are punishing to the performer).

As we said, people learn to avoid the things they are hit with.

In summary, when it appears that someone knows how to perform as desired but doesn't, find out whether the desired performance leads to unpleasant results (unpleasant from *his or her* point of view). If so, the remedy is to find ways to reduce or eliminate the negative effects and to create, or increase the strength of, positive or desirable consequences. (It is quite possible, of course, to offer an incentive for something that someone cannot be expected to do. Such unreasonable expectations can lead not only to frustration on the part of the person trying to perform, but to a feeling of failure—of being no good, of being "bad." Though a favorable consequence will increase the likelihood that desired actions *will* occur, or increase the frequency with which they do occur, it will only do so if the *desired* performance is *possible* performance. As the old saw says, "You can't make a silk purse out of a sow's ear unless you start with a silk sow.")

What to Do

Determine whether desired performance leads to unfavorable consequences.

How to Do It

Ask these questions:

- *What is the consequence of performing as desired?*
- *Is it punishing to perform as expected?*
- *Does the person perceive desired performance as being geared to penalties?*
- *Would the person's world become a little dimmer if the desired performance were attained?*

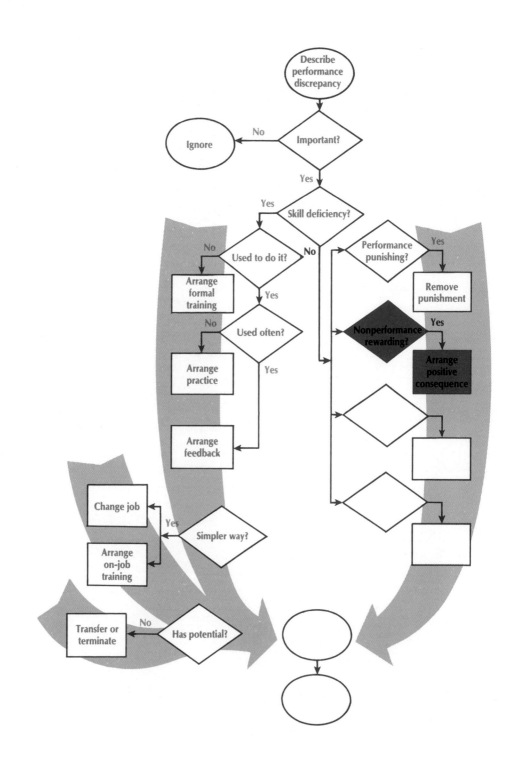

9 | Is Nonperformance Rewarding?

- **WHERE WE ARE**

An important discrepancy is known or suspected *not* to be due to a skill deficiency.

In the last chapter, we examined the fact that sometimes people don't do what they know how to do because the doing leads to unpleasant results. So, in analyzing a performance discrepancy that does not appear to be due to a skill deficiency, one step to take is to see if unpleasant consequences follow the desired performance. But there is another side to that issue. Performance may not be as expected because *non*performing is *rewarding*. That is, whether or not desired performance has favorable consequences, they are not as favorable as those of an other-than-desired performance. Thus, another step to take when looking for the cause of a "they-could-do-it-if-they-wanted-to-but-they-don't-and-they-oughta-wanna" problem is to explore the consequences of the thing they are doing *now*.

An office equipment manufacturer maintains a large staff of people whose task it is to repair customers' equipment when it goes belly-up. Their work is usually satisfactory, but at one point management noticed what was said to be a performance discrepancy.

"They just aren't doing their PM's," they said. A "PM" is a preventive maintenance routine involving dusting, adjusting, oiling, and replacement of suspiciously worn parts.

"We've sent them several memos, but they just don't do a PM when they should—every time they service a machine," said management.

It was puzzling, especially since "doing a PM" was good for the machine, good for company image and thus good for sales, and also good for the maintenance people. (PM's helped avoid the embarrassment of repeat calls.)

The problem was revealed when questions were asked about consequences.

"What happens if they *don't* do their PM's?" Well, the machine works just as well as it would otherwise, for the moment, and the service call takes less time.

"What happens if they *do* the PM as desired?" Well, then the service call takes a little longer. And though top management wanted the PM's done, the service managers were evaluating performance by counting the number of minutes spent on a service call. So to do the PM's (the desired performance) was to risk pay raises and promotions.

Two examples demonstrate people performing in ways that are other than desirable: the maternity ward receptionist who makes you fill out a dozen documents when it's obvious that the arrival of your child is imminent and the petty bureaucrat who counters all of your attempts to get something done with a regulation that says you can't, but who never offers a hint of the right course to follow.

If you take the view that these people are supposed to facilitate rather than obstruct, you have to assume that they are performing in an undesirable manner. Obstructive behavior must be more rewarding than facilitating behavior, even though the formal rewards of the job (pay, promotions) are apparently tied to the latter.

Push back at one of these functionaries and you will quickly be told, "I'm just doing my job. I don't make the rules."

Some of these misguided souls, finding no other satisfaction in their work, get satisfaction (attention?) from exerting petty tyranny over others. Others may be speaking the literal but partial truth when they say, "I'm just doing my job." They should add for the sake of accuracy, "... in a way that I perceive that my superiors want it done." Their perceptions may be far from accurate.

In all cases, something positive can be done. For petty tyrants, one has to find a way to make them glow for performing in the desirable way. (And since this may be hard to do, one may have to fall back on the last-but-not-least alternative: change the job or change the person.) For those who have an inaccurate picture of what their superiors want, there's plainly a need to spell out the true intent—to make sure they know what is to be done and can recognize when it has been done properly.

Here's a similar example: "We've got to teach that foreman to train his staff." (It's the production manager of a manufacturing company speaking.) "Training is his responsibility."

The foreman knew what his staff members needed to know, all right; but he didn't tell them, and production suffered.

Why didn't he do what needed to be done? What did he get out of keeping his staff ignorant?

Status! Anyone who wanted to know what was going on had to talk to the foreman. The foreman saw himself as cock of the roost; and, by keeping his subordinates uninformed, he thought he would stay that way. It was more rewarding (in *his* perception) not to perform as expected.

Solution? Not training. Make it *matter* to perform as desired.

And another example. In one of the large gold mines of Africa, the management once decided that they had a training problem involving African workers who operated the drilling rigs on the mine face. "We've got to teach these men to wear their earplugs," they said. The discussion with one of the managers went something like this:

"What happens if these men don't wear their earplugs?"
"Why, they go stone deaf from the unbelievable noise."
"Do they know *how* to wear their earplugs?"

"Of course. All they have to do is stick them into their ears."

"Do they have the plugs handy?"

"Yes. They carry them in their pockets. As a matter of fact, they are checked when they enter the mine to make sure they *do* have their earplugs with them."

"I see. So they know how to wear the plugs, and the plugs are always available?"

"That's right. But they don't wear them, and they really should."

"Why?"

"Why, to keep from going deaf, of course. Nobody oughta wanna go deaf."

"Do you have any idea why they *don't* wear their earplugs?"

"You know why they don't wear their earplugs? They don't wear their earplugs because this is the highest job an African can have in this mine . . . and he wears his deafness like a *status symbol.*"

Well, that put a new light on the problem. Then it was seen for what it was, a problem where performing as desired wasn't nearly as rewarding as performing otherwise. Loss of hearing was more desirable than loss of status. Notice again that all the training in the world is not likely to get those earplugs worn.

No doubt you can think of several possible solutions when the problem is posed in this manner: How can management make "being a driller" more visible to the outside world than deafness?

Situations like this aren't as rare as you might think. Though you may think it "unbelievable" that people would rather go deaf than wear earplugs, you can find similar examples if you just look around you. For example, ever heard of anyone who endured the pain of a malfunctioning tooth rather than go to a dentist? Or someone who would rather suffer the measles or mumps rather than tolerate a simple inoculation?

In working with a group of fire fighters on performance analysis issues, we learned of this little gem.

"They're supposed to wear their breathing apparatus when they go into a hot fire, but often they don't."

"What happens if they wear it, as they're supposed to?"

"Well, they complain that it's heavy, hard to see through the eyepieces, and clumsy to work with."

"And what happens if they *don't* wear the breathing apparatus?"

"If they don't wear it they have more mobility and can see better. And if they don't wear it, and *live*, they get to be known as 'old leatherlung', and that's real hero stuff."

Clearly a case of nonperformance (not wearing the apparatus) being more rewarding than performing as desired. Keep in mind that people respond to consequences whether they are aware of them or not. In other words, in most instances people don't *deliberately* nonperform. They simply do it because their world is more comfortable or pleasant that way than it is if they do it the way someone else says is the desired way.

It's a fact that there's a whole world out there just filled with people who are not doing as you would like. Not all are acting against your wishes because they don't know any better or because they don't know how to do differently. Most behave the way they do because they feel that *their* way leads to more favorable consequences for them than does *your* way. If you want them to do differently, you will have to invent a way to reverse things so that your way leads to the rosier results.

Why do you suppose all those people in the prisons of our land don't straighten up and live right when they are released? Certainly they know society *wants* them to do so, and many know *how* to do so. They also know it is important to do so if they are to avoid pursuit and arrest. But they don't. Why?

In some way their "contrary" behavior is more rewarding, has more payoff, leads to more desirable outcomes. When the pros and cons (steady there!) are weighed, the cons win out. There may be some undesirable consequences of a life of crime, of course; but, on balance, the advantages must be perceived by the criminal to outweigh the disadvantages.

This is an appropriate point to re-emphasize that problems of this kind do not always fall so neatly into categories as do our examples. Typically, problems have elements of more than one of the categories we have discussed, or they can move from one category to another.

In this chapter we have looked at cases where the consequences of undesired performance were more favorable than those that followed desired performance. Now consider this case. How often, when you have guests, do you rush over to where the kids are playing quietly in the corner and say, "Hey, kids, you're doing a *great* job of playing quietly in the corner"? Or do you, like most of us, wait until they start acting up and *then* rush over to scold?*

One can argue that you are, at best, providing no consequence for desired behavior. There may be favorable results for playing quietly in the corner, but *you* aren't the source of them.

A gloomier view of the situation is this: If *attention from parent* is viewed by your child as desirable, what must he or she do to get it? When you ignore episodes of peace and quiet but attend to the uproars, you strengthen the likelihood that you will be confronted by an uproar.

An old expression fits here: It's the squeaky wheel that gets the grease. Might not this be why people feel that to get action they must do something other than behave in a manner resembling "sitting quietly in the corner"?

We're not suggesting, by the way, that you "spoil" your children by refraining from admonition when they misbehave. We are only making the point that when you forget to "glow after good" as well as "growl after bad," you run the risk of making the growl a rosier consequence than you intend.

Consider the example set by "Ol' Boney."

"Our department has a dozen truck drivers. They're all safe drivers, except one, and he costs about two thousand per year in property damage and ill will. We never know when he's going to hit somebody. And he's also erratic in his private

---

* Our thanks to Lloyd Homme for this example.

driving, as his record shows. He's run over a gas pump, run over a customer's wet concrete, and so on."

"Is it a skill deficiency, do you think?"

"No, because most months his driving is perfect."

"Hmm. What happens when he *does* have an accident?"

"Then he gets a lot of attention from his cronies. They gather around him and ask him to recount the episode while they chuckle. 'Ol' Boney's done it again,' they'll say, and he gets to tell it again."

"By the way, what happens to your good drivers?"

"What do you mean?"

"What is the consequence of having a good driving record?"

"We don't do anything special for good drivers; that's what we *expect* of them."

"Oh."

Even our educational establishment is loaded with examples of conditions or consequences that make someone's world brighter for *not* performing as you wish.

Let's begin with an analogy. Suppose that while walking in the park you come upon a man standing in front of two plants and muttering to himself. He is using a watering can to water one of the plants. You ask him what he is doing.

"I'm trying to make *that* one grow," he replies, and points to the *other* one.

"Well," you might ask, puzzled, "if you want *that* one to grow, why are you watering *this* one?"

"Because the other one oughta wanna grow anyhow!"

Wacky? Of course. Yet this is very much like the way our school system is operated.

The chief goal of a school is to help students' capabilities grow—to change their state of knowledge, skill, and understanding. Thus, the measure of success is the degree to which the students' capabilities are increased. Since student performance is what is desired, one would think that the rewards of the system (money, raises, position, status) would be strongly tied to teaching excellence. Yet this appears not to be the case. Look at the salary schedule of nearly every school and you will find that the rewards (favorable consequences) of the system have little direct relationship to effective teaching. Raises and promotions are based almost exclusively on the number of months served and the number of academic credit hours earned. There is little or no attempt to tie these rewards for the teacher to the quantity and quality of student performance.

In these circumstances, to say that teachers oughta wanna teach more effectively is to behave like the nut with the watering can—it is demanding one kind of performance while rewarding another.

The situation is even more bizarre at the university level. Here professors get promotions and raises not on how well they succeed with students, but on the basis of how much they publish, how many government grants they are able to garner, and the number of committees on which they serve. Again, they are exhorted to do one thing while being rewarded for another.

Since people tend to do those things that brighten their world, the moral is:

Water the performance you want to grow.

Think for a moment about the expression "resistance to change." It's a judgment often made about people who don't perform as desired. But the expression is misleading, because it puts a derogatory emphasis where it doesn't belong. When people oppose the introduction of some new idea or thing, there usually isn't an *active* resistance in force. Often, people cling to the old because there is *no real reason*, no favorable consequence to *them*, for doing it the new way. It is more comfortable, more pleasant, more rewarding to stay with the old. So here again, simply plying people with information about the new thing or exhorting them that they oughta wanna be in favor of newness may not change much. The desired performance (the new thing) will be more readily adopted (and made to work during any "teething troubles") if it is plain to the doer how it will make his or her world brighter.

In much the same way, the teacher passes the blame for his or her own failure to be interesting by complaining about students' "short attention spans." It would be much better if he or she approached the problem by asking, "What's the consequence to the student who does pay attention?" If the honest answer is "boredom," then there isn't much doubt where the remedy lies.

One more category can be listed here. Let's call it the "don't-let's-stick-our-necks-out-more-than-we-have-to" category. It's found at many levels in the working world and in private life, and can be found under at least two subheadings—the mental version and the physical version.

A typical instance of the first is found in people who apparently "don't like to take responsibility." These are often people who have discovered that when they make a wrong decision, they get it in the neck. And if they get it in the neck often enough and hard enough, they're going to conclude that one way of shutting off aversive consequences is to make *fewer* of these decisions. Eventually, they establish an equilibrium, making as few decisions as it is possible to make without getting genuine complaints that they're loafing.

You can think of your own examples of students who try but get poor grades, and children who seem reluctant to do chores.

That's the mental aspect of the problem. The physical aspect is similar. Some activities are physically exacting; the more a person does, the more tired he or she gets. When getting excessively tired leads to no positive consequence, the doer finds a point of equilibrium.

When someone is exhibiting these symptoms, people may say, "He's a good man, but . . . ." Or, leaping sprightly to conclusions, they judge: "She's not ambitious." "He doesn't care." "She procrastinates." Or worst of all, "He's lazy."

The people judged may not like to act this way. But, as they see the world, the less they do, the less they have to answer for or the less they suffer. The consequence—or, more accurately in most cases, the sum of the consequences—for doing more was not worth the effort.

Maybe they don't have the mental or physical stuff to perform as you would like. But if you're the one in charge of the consequences that come to them as a result of action or nonaction, maybe you should take a close look at those consequences to make sure they are worthy of the effort you are expecting.

What to Do

Determine whether non*performance or* other *performance leads to more favorable consequences than would desired performance.*

How to Do It

Ask these questions:

- *What is the result of doing it the present way instead of my way?*

- *What does the person get out of the present performance in the way of reward, prestige, status, jollies?*

- *Does the person get more attention for misbehaving than for behaving?*

- *What event in the world supports (rewards) the present way of doing things? (Am I inadvertently rewarding irrelevant behavior while overlooking the crucial behaviors?)*

- *Is this person "mentally inadequate," doing less so that there is less to worry about?*

- *Is this person physically inadequate, doing less because it is less tiring?*

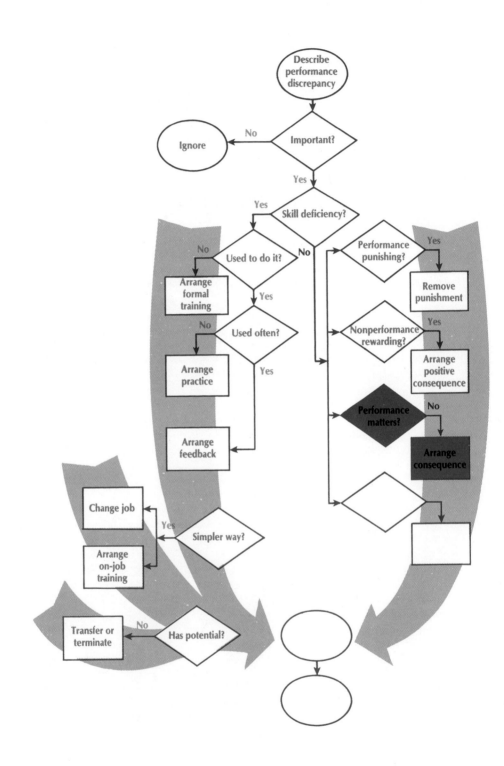

10 Does Performing Really Matter to Them?

■ WHERE WE ARE

An important discrepancy is known or suspected *not* to be due to a skill deficiency.

Sometimes a performance discrepancy continues to exist *neither* because performers don't know how to perform *nor* because they aren't motivated, but because it simply makes no difference to them whether they perform or not. There are no consequences to them if they take the trouble to perform, and no consequences to them for not doing it.

The laws of behavior tell us that when a performance is not followed at least periodically by an event considered favorable by the performer, that performance will tend to disappear. If there is no consequence to make it worth doing, it will tend not to get done.

An important point (because few people seem to grasp it): Wagging your forefinger at someone and telling him or her, "You oughta wanna," does *not* qualify as a universal incentive to action.

A common instance of this cause of a performance discrepancy comes from that generally unpleasant area known as paperwork. Managers complain, "Reports just don't get in on time," or "Those reports are haphazardly done."

In such instances, the conversation continues like this:

"The reports are sloppily done?"

"They certainly are. And they don't come in on time."

"Why not, do you suppose?"

"Staff members just don't seem to care!"

"What happens if the reports are late?"

"Well, then I have to explain to my superiors why I am late with *my* reports."

"No, no. What happens to the people who submit the reports?"

"Well, nothing, I guess. But they oughta wanna get them in on time."

"What happens if the reports are sloppily done?"

"Disaster! My poor secretary works like mad trying to get them cleaned up in time to attach to my own report."

"Yes, but what happens to the people who send in the sloppy work?"

"Well, nothing, I guess."

"You don't phone them or drop them a memo to tell them they have not met expected standards?"

"No."

"You don't send the reports back for *them* to correct?"

"Heavens, no. There's never *time*."

"So it doesn't really matter *to the staff members* whether their reports are well done and on time?"

"No, I guess not. But they oughta wanna do them right."

Let's not get caught up in a debate about the importance of paperwork. The example is intended to illustrate that desired performance is less likely to be attained when that performance does not "matter" to the performer—that is, when the performance does not lead to consequences considered favorable by the performer.

Police departments seem to be as good a source of "no-consequence" examples as business and industry. In one such department, patrol teams were required to take their batons (bopping sticks) with them whenever they got out of the patrol car. Apparently this wasn't happening all the time, and so the captain asked the trainer to add something to the instruction that would "teach patrol officers to have the right attitude" about baton handling.

The officers, however, already *knew* they were to take their batons with them. So why didn't they do it? Well, a baton is a stiff, hard item that can cause pain if it isn't removed from the belt ring before entering a patrol car (or any other car, for that matter). As a result, there is a tendency to remove the baton from the belt ring and place it on the seat. On leaving a car, officers may have to take their hats, a clipboard, or perhaps a shotgun, and once in a while there is a tendency to forget the batons.

But consider the consequences to the officers. What happened to them if they took their batons with them (the desired performance)? Nothing much. They had them when they needed them, but that was seldom. What happened if they left them in the car most of the time? Nothing much. Besides, if the radio call described a situation that sounded like a head-thumper, they didn't forget to take them along.

In yet another department, patrol car drivers were expected to keep their own cars clean. As they weren't too diligent about that chore, management would periodically complain and tack memos onto the bulletin board. When the expectation was looked at in terms of consequences, favorable responses were again lacking. If drivers kept the cars clean, nobody said anything. If drivers didn't, management nagged. As most people learn to tune out nagging, it hardly qualifies as a meaningful consequence. Without consequences, why should anyone expect the performance to be different from what it is?

The solution to this "problem" was simple. The police department contracted with a local car wash to wash and clean patrol cars whenever they appeared. Drivers were told to run through the car wash whenever they had spare time. As that was easy to do, the problem was solved.

In this example, a manager was discussing the people who work at the serving window of a fast-food chain.

"When taking orders, these window people are supposed to ask whether the customer wants any of the various extras. But most of the time they forget."
"What's the result?"
"The result is that our sales are less than they might be, and customers aren't reminded about items they may really want."
"What's the result to the window people? What happens to *them* if they forget to tout the extras?"
"Well, we can't afford to stand over their shoulders and tell them every time they forget."
"Does anything *ever* happen to them when they don't do as you want?"
"No, I guess not."

No consequence for doing it right, and none for doing it wrong—and thus, no real urgency for behaving differently. Solution? List all the possible ways of making the order-takers' world a little brighter when performing as desired. Then select one or more that are practical and less expensive than the problem, and that would be seen as favorable by the recipients of the consequence(s).

And here's a common "problem" solved by ingenuity. A professor kept urging his students to "sit down front" when attending lectures and demonstrations in the tiered classroom. But students continued to sit in the back. "If you sit in the front," the professor would tell the students, "I won't have to talk so loudly." But they still sat in the back.

Someone finally hit on an idea—it was adopted and the problem was solved. The solution? The first five rows of seats were upholstered; the remaining rows were left with hardwood chairs. Then almost everyone tried to get to class early so they could sit down front.

Here's another success story, engineered by a Midwestern florist who noticed that many hospital nurses frequently went without recognition for their efforts. Whenever he sent flowers to a hospital patient, he always enclosed a single, separate carnation with a card saying, "For your favorite nurse."

Nurses who received them (including the men) pinned them on their uniforms, and in the cafeteria there was always conversation about "Whose favorite nurse are you?"

As one of the nurses explained, "Usually, the only way for a patient to express gratitude is with a 'Thank you' at the end of a stay. This way, everybody was a winner. Nurses got recognition. The patient was still around to receive more of the TLC. And it didn't hurt the florist's business, either."

Meanwhile, nearer home, you have undoubtedly heard your neighbor complain that her daughter simply will not pick up after herself, no matter how often she is told. If you were to listen to a conversation between this parent and someone skilled in the use of our checklist, you might hear:

"She doesn't pick up after herself, even though you've made it clear you expect her to?"

"I've told her and I've told her, but it doesn't do any good."

"And she knows where to put the clothes?"

"Of *course* she does. She isn't stupid, you know."

"Sorry. Ah, tell me—what is the result of her not picking up after herself?"

"The result? The result is that I spend half *my* time picking up after her. *That's* the result!"

"I understand. But what's the result to *her*?"

"I nag."

"And how about if she does pick up?"

"What do you mean?"

"Does something favorable happen if she picks up after herself for a certain period of time—like an extra movie, or a round of applause from the family, or a favorite meal, or something else she might like to have?"

"Certainly *not*! You don't think I'm going to *bribe* her to do something she oughta wanna do anyhow, do you?"

[*Bribe* is a loaded word, carrying a connotation of something illegal or designed to make someone do something against his or her will, breaking moral laws. But bribery is a concept having to do with ethics rather than with the laws of behavior. What we're talking about is a *positive consequence* that, if you like loaded words, could as well be called a *reward*. By providing a positive consequence, you increase the probability that behavior will occur. Even when you do something you don't like to do (when, say, you submit to surgery), you do it because you expect that life will be improved as a result. But you don't look on "getting better as a result of surgery" as a bribe. When a mother says to her child, "If you pick up your clothes for a week, I'll take you to a movie," it is not bribery. It is the offer of an incentive (a consequence desired by the child) in return for performance desired by the mother.]

In this case, the performance discrepancy is that the youngster doesn't pick up her clothes in the desired manner with the desired regularity. She knows how to do it, but she doesn't do it. Thus, the discrepancy is not likely to be eliminated by training or instruction. Her world doesn't get brighter if she does as expected; and, since she's so used to being nagged that she doesn't even hear it, her world doesn't get dimmer if she doesn't. In effect, nothing meaningful happens one way or the other. There is no consequence for performing as desired, so she tends not to.

Again, it is easy to say that she oughta wanna pick up after herself because it is the adult thing, the right thing, the moral thing, the mother-saving thing, etc. And some day, probably, she *will* pick up after herself, because it matters to her self-concept or her convenience to do so. But right now there are none of these *internal* consequences. If the mother expects her daughter to perform, then she must see to it that the child's performance is followed by an *external* consequence that has value for *the child*.

Another interesting example is found in the inspection departments of some manufacturing companies. One of the duties is that of inspecting incoming materials. In one such

plant, the features to be evaluated include the smoothness of various metal surfaces. The inspector checks to see if the smoothness meets or surpasses specifications. If it does, the material is accepted and sent on to the production department. If not smooth enough, the material is returned to the vendor.

It was noticed that inspectors were rejecting material that was, in fact, smooth enough to be accepted. "We have a training problem," said a manager. "We need to teach these inspectors to be more accurate in their smoothness judgments."

By now you are probably ahead of us and know that training wasn't the solution.

To the question, "What is the consequence of performing as desired?", a double answer appeared. To the inspectors, the result of rejecting a good batch was nothing. The batch went back to the vendor; and the vendor, knowing the game, probably let it sit in the warehouse for a month or so and then resubmitted it. On the other hand, accepting a bad batch brought the wrath of the production department down on an inspector's head.

Thus, there was no noticeable consequence of rejecting a good batch of material (undesirable performance), but it was punishing to accept a bad batch of material (also undesirable performance). The result was that the inspectors, without even realizing it, gradually rejected more and more good batches in order to avoid the punishment that came with accepting a bad one. This was not a conscious action; it just happened.

There are a number of options for correcting this kind of problem. Management could act to make both undesirable alternatives equally undesirable to the inspectors. Since the inspectors *want* to perform well, one could also make the accuracy of their performance more immediately visible to them. If inspectors knew they were making a bad decision, they wouldn't make it. In this case, performance feedback would probably do the trick.

Actually, however, a third alternative was selected, mostly because of the awkwardness and time needed in providing immediate feedback. Since this situation turned out to be a combination of a skill maintenance and a no-consequence problem, a little device was constructed with which the inspectors could periodically check their smoothness perceptions. The device provided a number of graded samples for inspectors to judge, and then told them whether they were right or wrong. They weren't learning anything they didn't already know, but they *were* keeping their skill sharpened. It would also have helped to equalize the consequence for either of the undesired performances (accepting a bad batch or rejecting a good one), or to have increased the consequence of good performance. But to our knowledge this was not arranged.

As mentioned elsewhere, many discrepancies have elements of more than one cause; this was one such example.

Examples of "no-consequence" situations are all around us.

"The manager is not walking the store."
"The manager isn't delegating."
"Employees don't show enough courtesy to customers."
"Meat cutters aren't cutting the meat right."

In every one of these examples (from our files) the answers to the consequence questions were negative. It didn't matter whether a performance was done in the desired manner or in some other manner. Oh, it mattered to *somebody*, all right, or the problem wouldn't have become visible. But the mattering didn't consist of consequences that impinge on the performers themselves. Whenever you hear any of the following,

"They should do it because it's good for the company"
"Our image will suffer if they don't _____"
"What will the neighbors think if you don't _____?"
"All hell breaks loose here when you don't _____"
"It's the patriotic thing to do"
"It's the professional thing to do"
"They just don't seem to realize how their actions affect others,"

you are hearing descriptions of situations in which the consequences or results, large though they may be to *someone*, are probably not having any effect on those at whom the finger is being pointed.

During a workshop on performance analysis, two pleasant women recounted an experience they described as "delicious." They began:

"Among other things, we're responsible for duplicating professors' tests by the deadlines set for the examinations. Most of the professors bring in their items in enough time for us to do the duplication without any trouble. Only one was always late."

"What happened when he was late?"

"Oh, then we had to drop everything at the last minute, and we had to be late with some of our work. It was very exasperating."

"But what was the consequence to the professor?"

"Ahh, but *that's* the point. We finally figured out that *we* were experiencing all the consequences. So the very next time he brought his items in late, we said, 'Sorry, professor, but your items are too late to include in the test,' and went on about our business. Well, you should have seen him! Practically had a tantrum. Ranted and raved, got all flushed in the face. But you know what?"

"No. What?"

"He has *never, ever* been late since!"

Once they understood the problem (no consequences *to the professor* for undesired performance), the solution was clear. Make it matter *to the performers*; arrange consequences.

When hunting for consequences that follow desired and undesired performance, be sure to keep in mind that it is the consequences to the performers that matter rather than the consequences to the boss, the parent, the organization, or the economy. It is the perception of the performers that matters; how *they* see it is what controls the outcome.

That important point was brought home to us again during a discussion with the chief neurosurgeon of a large hospital. He was describing the time he had decided to offer a series of afternoon lectures to medical aides. He wanted to help them understand the larger picture—*why* they were taking blood pressure, blood samples, and so forth—so that they might feel more a part of the treatment team. A noble mission, and yet . . . Listen to how it turned out.

"About 40 showed up for the first lecture, and every one of them seemed eager for the information. Many of them gathered around me to ask questions when the lecture was over.

"Only about half of them showed up for the second lecture. Again, they all seemed eager and asked lots of questions.

"Only half of *them*, about ten, showed up for the third lecture. As before, they all seemed eager and asked questions. But I couldn't understand why attendance was cut in half each time. So I asked the head nurse what happened to them.

"'They quit!' was the reply.

"Quit? But *why?*

"'Well, when they finally realized the importance of what they were doing, they quit to avoid the heavy responsibility.'"

Here was an instance in which desired performance wasn't perceived as punishing until the aides learned the "whys" of their work. So never mind whether *you* perceive the consequences as rewarding—what matters is how the performer perceives it.

In summary, when you're dealing with a case where it looks as though a person *could* perform if he or she had to or wanted to, one of the things to look for is the *consequence* of doing it. If there *isn't any*—at least if there isn't any that is considered favorable by the person expected to perform differently—then the remedy that suggests itself is to arrange one.

When you want someone to perform in some particular manner, one rule is:

Make it matter.

What to Do

Determine whether there is a meaningful consequence for the desired performance.

How to Do It

Ask these questions:

- *Does performing as desired matter to the performer?*
- *Is there a favorable outcome for performing?*
- *Is there an undesirable outcome for not performing?*
- *Is there a source of satisfaction for performing?*
- *Can the person take pride in this performance as an individual or as a member of a group?*
- *Is there satisfaction of personal needs from the job?*

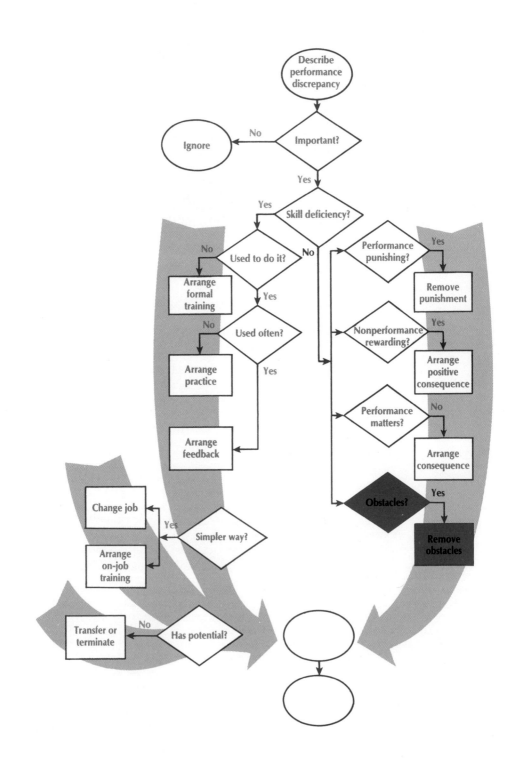

11 || Are There Obstacles to Performing?

- WHERE WE ARE

An important discrepancy is known or suspected *not* to be due to a skill deficiency.

If the person knows how to do it, isn't doing it, but ought to do it, there are four general causes to look for:

1. It's punishing to do it.
2. It's rewarding *not* to do it.
3. It doesn't matter whether he or she does it.
4. There are obstacles to doing it.

We have discussed the first three; now we'll consider the issue of obstacles.

Have you ever said to yourself, "I could do this job perfectly well if only the !?#$%#?! telephone would stop ringing and those idiots next door would stop pestering me so that I could concentrate for five minutes at a time!"

That's a perfect example of a situation in which a job would get done more efficiently if the conditions were changed—without the need for instruction. It's a typical problem for people in all walks of life. The victim would do an acceptable job, if only he or she could get *at* the job. Some are more stoical about this than others, of course. The lower

105

people are in the pecking order, the more likely it is that they'll tolerate an obstacle, since they are not in the happy position of being able to tell the boss, "Quit bugging me!"

We know that in industry it is courting inefficiency, if not disaster, to organize in a way that gives a person more than one boss. Inevitably it happens that in trying to please one, he or she must neglect the interests of others. Multiple-bossism is recognized as bad management. Yet in our schools students have as many bosses as they have teachers, each putting demands upon their time and attention and, frequently, each imposing different rules. When some students fail to meet the demands and follow the rules, unfavorable consequences follow. And eventually these students can end up saying, "I hate school."

Now this is not to say that no student ever goofed off. But it does indicate that we might get more from students (and students might get more satisfaction from school) if we paid more heed to the conditions under which they are expected to perform.

Teachers, too, are prevented from doing a better job by the conditions under which they work. Too often, the teacher is expected to collect milk money, keep interminable records, and otherwise devote considerable time to chores just as well handled at a clerical level. We have talked to teachers in many colleges who are expected to use films, slides, and other visual materials freely. But the equipment and help they need are available only from a remote (but oh-so-central) location, through a flurry of paperwork administered by an office that is not always open for business when the teacher can go there.

Here are some other examples.

In a large supermarket, the manager noted that stockers were stocking (placing merchandise on the shelves) only 60 cases per hour, when they should have been stocking 90 cases per hour. After some discussion about the cause of the discrepancy, it finally occurred to the manager to ask the stockers if *they* had any idea why they weren't stocking the standard amount.

"Geez," they said. "You want 90 cases an hour? You got it."

The only thing standing in the way of desired performance was information telling them exactly what that performance *was*.

One of our colleagues tells this story.

"I'd always wanted to play golf, so I took a course in college. They taught me how to hold a club, how to swing, and I was all set. And yet, after the course ended, it was *two years* before I actually played on a public course."

"What stopped you?" we asked.

"They didn't teach me how to *get onto* a golf course, and I was embarrassed at the thought of not knowing the ropes."

It may seem like a small obstacle to you, but it kept our friend from enjoying the sport he's enjoyed ever since.

PP:	Bob, didn't you have a similar experience with your dancing lessons?
RFM:	Yes. When I decided to take tap lessons just a few years ago, it was six weeks before I could screw up the courage to call a dance studio.
PP:	What prevented you?
RFM:	It wasn't skill—I knew how to look up a number and use the phone. It was the thought of this grey-haired man clomping around amongst a bevy of leotard-clad little girls that stopped me. When I *did* finally look in the phone book, it was another six weeks before I selected a number to call.
PP:	And when you finally gathered the courage to call?
RFM:	Once I called it was smooth sailing. But the lack of knowledge about what to expect was a real obstacle, and the way the ads were written just made it worse.

It's no good to just sit there thinking, "That was no obstacle, that was just stupidity. All he had to do was call and get the information he needed." Remember Cram's law: People don't do things for the darnedest reasons.* People are not necessarily *aware* of why they aren't doing something they know how to do. They simply don't do it. If they don't *know* that one of their habits is offensive to others, they don't do it another way. If lack of information keeps them from approaching situations they might otherwise get involved in, it doesn't change matters to charge them with "stupidity." After all, if people aren't *aware* of their lack of knowledge (obstacle)—that is, if they don't know that a lack of information is preventing them from doing something—the charge that they are stupid is no more helpful than to say they "really oughta wanna" change.

Another type of obstacle is that of procedure, routine, or what may be referred to as "the way it's done here." How many times have you been astonished to learn that something takes a lot longer than necessary because of the paperwork, the number of steps that must be followed, or the number of approvals that must be sought?

When one of our largest retail chains installed computers at the checkout counters, it was noted that it took about one-third *longer* to buy something than it did before the computer was installed. Why? Well, instead of taking your money, issuing a receipt, and sending you on your way to spend money in other parts of the store, the clerk is required to make you stand there while he or she punches key after key, entering administrative information of no relevance to the transaction between you and the store. Information that will be used for inventory control is punched in, along with numbers that will be used for reasons having nothing to do with taking your money and issuing a receipt. Why don't the store employees do all that on their *own* time and send you off to spend elsewhere?

---

* Periodically muttered by Dr. David Cram, who also *does* things for the darnedest reasons.

Who knows? But the bulky procedure they use is clearly an obstacle to increased sales.

Do you avoid shopping at some stores because there's never anyone around to help? Because you can never find a clerk to answer questions, so you can never find what you want? What obstacles to the desired performance (for the store) of "increased sales"!

When the first retail computer stores were opened, the sales staffs were composed largely of computer programmers. Someone had decided that programmers were the only ones who knew enough about the products to sell them. The result, though, was largely exasperating to the customer. Customers could stand there waving a fistful of money until closing time and never be noticed, because the "sales" staff was busy playing at terminals. The customers knew how to give clerks the money, so there was not a skill deficiency involved. There was, however, a large obstacle to customers performing as the store management would have liked.

Imagine yourself being called in by the personnel director of a French department store and being asked to solve a training problem. Specifically, you are asked to develop a sales course for clerks. At this point you have no information about *why* the course is needed (you don't know whether there are performance discrepancies, and if so, how large they are), and so you don't know *whether* instruction is needed. Clearly, more information is needed about why the director thinks instruction is needed.

On questioning, he reveals that he wants sales training because "gross receipts are not what they should be".

Now the amount of money taken in by a store is only partly related to the skill of its salesclerks. Since in further questioning the director said nothing directly related to salesclerks and their abilities, we began to wonder if the cause of the problem might be elsewhere. We asked to be shown around the store. Within a few minutes, we noted several clumps of people gathered around cash registers trying to give the clerks money to complete transactions. Then we found that some merchandise was placed on the counters according to manufacturer rather than according to type. If you wanted to look at transistor radios, for example, you might first go to the Phillips department to see what they had, and then walk to the Telefunken department (some distance away) to see what they had there.

In some ways, this is typical of the situations wrongly labeled "training problems." Basically, what is wrong is that management has rushed to a solution without first looking at other elements of the problem. Here, as in most situations involving those infinitely variable entities called people, there is probably no perfect solution to yield a perfect answer. But there are usually some solutions that are superior to others in terms of return for effort expended.

It's not too much to say that the management of this store singled out the element that was most visible and most under its control and made it the scapegoat for an important discrepancy. They then identified a solution that involved changing the salesclerks in some way.

The trouble with premature identification of solutions is that it blocks off exploration of other problem elements. We tend to say to ourselves, "Well, that's that. We've nailed down what we're going to do. Now let's get on with doing it." Because we feel "We're doing something about it," some of the burden of the problem has been lifted from our shoulders.

It's probably clear, however, that other elements contributed to the store's problem. In studying the procedures, it became plain that the store's merchandising policies almost seemed designed to prevent customers from buying; or, having once bought, to discourage them from coming back again. It was hard to find what one wanted. It was hard to complete a purchase. Once the merchandising procedures were revised and the time to complete a transaction was reduced, sales increased.

The training director of a dynamite factory overseas told of an instance where all the training in the world would have been useless in solving the problem.

He was called by a plant manager. "I've got a training problem," said the manager. "These people are lazy. Many fall asleep on the job, and they don't come to work regularly. I want you to come up here and teach them their jobs. I want you to teach them to be motivated."

The training director was too smart to fall into the trap of taking a statement like that at face value, especially since it began with the usual confusion of problem with solution. Knowing his human relations, he replied, "I'll come and take a look around so that I can see more clearly what needs to be taught." (It doesn't get you very far to tell a client that his or her diagnosis is probably wrong. It works better to agree that there is a problem and then do your analysis out loud, hoping that *the client* will spot the difficulty.)

The training director went to the site, looked around, talked to people, and reviewed employee records. All the while, he was asking himself whether he was dealing with a skill deficiency—and, if not, why the men were not performing as expected.

He found the answer in an unexpected place—the medical office. Better than 60 percent of the employees in question were suffering from a disease that shows up in symptoms of sleeping sickness. *Of course* these men were falling asleep on the job. *Of course* their attendance was spotty.

But there wasn't anything wrong with their skill or with their motivation. They were simply sick. Once cured, all was well. Until those medical records were checked, though, no one even guessed that the obstacle to performing as desired was physiological.

Again, all the training in the world would not have done much good. Had the training director simply done what he was asked, his training program would have failed. Then the plant manager might have said, "Why spend all this money on a training department? We'd be better off without 'em." And what's more, if the training department continually used training as a solution for the wrong problems, he'd be right.

Thus, if performance discrepancies appear *not* to be due to a lack of skill or motivation, one thing to look for is the *obstacle*. "I can't do it" isn't always just an alibi; it can be an accurate description of the situation. And if you will look around to see what might be obstructing performance, you will find the solution to at least some of your performance problems.

Obstacles can take many forms and, as illustrated by the case of the dynamite workers, may appear in unlikely places. A few years ago, one of us was asked to review a division of a company and make whatever recommendations for improvement seemed appropriate. Things were going pretty well, so this was not one of the instances that begins with "I've got a training problem." Production was down a little, but it was not a matter of panic proportions, although puzzling.

As is customary, two or three days were spent soaking in the activities of the division, working from inspectors of incoming material toward the loading dock.

It was learned that though production was sagging, nothing else had changed. There was no new product that people had to learn how to build. The same employees were still on the scene. There were no new, complicated machines to master. There seemed to be no morale or personality problems of any significance. Parts were flowing smoothly to the supply bins located at one end of the production floor. Tools were plentiful and in good working order.

Then what?

The answer, the ridiculous answer, was discovered while sitting with some spotwelders at their workbenches. It was noticed that they were rather slow in getting up to refill the empty parts bins on their benches. Why? They were one stool short on the production floor! Getting up meant that a welder's stool might be gone when she returned. So each woman dawdled when her bins were empty, and each spent time carving her initials or taping identifying marks on "her" stool.

For want of a stool . . . . Clearly there was an obstacle to desired performance.

Another form of obstacle to desired performance that is seldom identified as such is that of absence of information about what is wanted. If people don't *know* that they are expected to perform in some way, they may fail to do so, even though they know how to do so. At the risk of offending a

small minority, we will generalize that nobody can read minds. If you want people to perform in a particular way, let them in on the secret. Tell them what is expected, and what the standards are. Note the examples that follow.

The Case of the Secret Agenda

The secret agenda is too common in industry. It often shows up in discussions with the bewildered employee who has just been demoted or booted clear off the payroll.

"What did you do that got you fired?", one might ask.

And you might receive a reply like this: "I don't know! I honestly don't know. My performance reviews were all favorable . . . and my boss kept telling me I was doing a good job. Then, all of a sudden, I was fired. I honestly don't know why."

Although it is probably true that some employees pretend ignorance of the reason for their sudden separation, it would be foolish to assume that all of them are being deceitful. More likely it never occurred to others to tell the employees what was expected of them; or perhaps those in charge were not mature enough to inform them of what they were doing to cause the displeasure of the establishment.

The Case of the Hidden Hatchet

A large company recently took a look at its course for management trainees. When the course was analyzed for effectiveness, it was noted that some trainees were let go at the end of instruction even though their technical performance was good or adequate. When we asked why, we were told it was because these trainees manifested some personal characteristics considered inappropriate for an executive.

Had these characteristics ever been brought to the attention of the trainees so that they might have a chance to change them? No. Why not? Because it is hard to tell a man that you don't like the color of his ties, or a woman that her blue jeans are offensive. It is easier to tell people that they are not suitable for the job, or to mumble something about performance, and drop the hatchet.

The course now includes a personality checklist that the training supervisor *must* fill out and show the trainees each month. In this way, trainees who exhibit behaviors considered objectionable by management will have an opportunity to change if they so desire.

The Case of the Elusive Evaluation

The faculty of a medical school once complained, "These students of ours will argue for hours over half a point on our written exams. Yet it isn't the *written* exams that are important. We've got to teach them to be less concerned with those darned paper-and-pencil tests." The rest of the conversation went like this:

"The students really care about their performance on the written tests?"

"Yes. And they shouldn't. It's the *subjective* evaluations the staff makes of the students that are important."

"When is this evaluation made?"

"All day and every day our staff members are noting and evaluating each student's actual performance. We note how he or she performs with patients in the clinic, with other students, and with staff, as well as noting performance in the lab."

"How do you consolidate the results of these subjective evaluations?"

"We compare notes."

"Who does?"

"The staff. We get together and discuss the progress of each student."

"Is the student present?"

"Certainly not."

"So the results of the written exams are *visible* to students, but the results of subjective evaluations are *in*visible to them?"

"Yes. But visible or not, it's the subjective evaluations that are really important; and that's what students ought to be interested in."

You can imagine how difficult it was to refrain from asking point-blank, "If they're *that* important, why keep them such a big secret?"

The Case of the Masticating Menace

We met a man highly competent and creative in his field who, we were told, is avoided by friends and business associates alike. Associates dread having to take him along to meet clients if a meal is involved, because he chomps his food with his mouth open—and talks while doing so. He's done it for years, and for years people have avoided taking him to business meals. So far, nobody has had the nerve—or the consideration—to tell him about it.

So why should he change?

How many executives have been fired, kicked upstairs, or retired because their superiors had the position but not the guts to tell them about an offensive but easy-to-correct habit?

How many teachers must there be who return test results to students days, even weeks, after the test was taken, and who then complain that student performance isn't any better than it is—and that the students don't seem to care?

Might your relations with others improve if you could know how they really feel about your present words and actions? Would you be willing to give up using a particular expression, or a gesture, if you knew it was offensive to someone you cared about?

Closely related to not knowing *that* you are expected to do something is not knowing *when* you are expected to do it. For example, a physical scientist working in the laboratory of a rather large corporation confided that he had been rated down by his boss because of what the boss referred to as an "undesirable characteristic." The conversation went like this.

"My boss said I didn't know how to keep my mouth shut."

"And *can* you?"

"Of *course* I can. Discretion is the name of the game in the lab I work in. If I couldn't keep my mouth shut, I'd have been out of a job long ago."

"Then what do you suppose the boss is complaining about?"

"Well, every once in a while he calls me into a meeting and asks me to tell them what I *really* think about something or other. And I do."

"And that's bad?"

"Only sometimes. Occasionally there is someone sitting in the meeting from another division, or even from a customer's company, and I'm not aware of it. *Then* when my boss asks what I really think, he seems to want me to say something to make the company look good rather than to tell him what I really think. Trouble is . . . I can never tell when to do which."

Thus, if a person is unable to tell *when* to perform in a particular way, if the signal isn't recognizable, somebody might conclude that the person doesn't know *how*.

In summary, if it looks as though people know how to perform but don't perform, look for obstacles. Look for things that might be getting in the way of their performing as desired. Look for their lack of authority, lack of time, or lack of tools. Look for poorly placed or poorly labeled equipment. Look for bad lighting and uncomfortable surroundings. Look for lack of *direct* information about *what* to do and *when* to do it. Above all, keep in mind that if they *can* do it but aren't doing it, there is a reason; and only seldom is the reason either a lack of interest or a lack of motivation or desire. Most people want to do a good job. When they don't, it is often because of an obstacle in the world around them.

What to Do

Determine whether there are obstacles preventing the desired performance.

How to Do It

Ask these questions:

- *What prevents this person from performing?*
- *Does the person know what is expected?*
- *Does the person know when to do what is expected?*
- *Are there conflicting demands on this person's time?*
- *Does the person lack*
  ... the authority?
  ... the time?
  ... the tools?
- *Are there restrictive policies, or a "right way of doing it," or a "way we've always done it" that ought to be changed?*
- *Can I reduce interference by*
  ... improving lighting?
  ... changing colors?
  ... increasing comfort?
  ... modifying the work position?
  ... reducing visual or auditory distractions?
- *Can I reduce "competition from the job"—phone calls, "brush fires," demands of less important but more immediate problems?*

PART
IV

What Should
I Do Now?

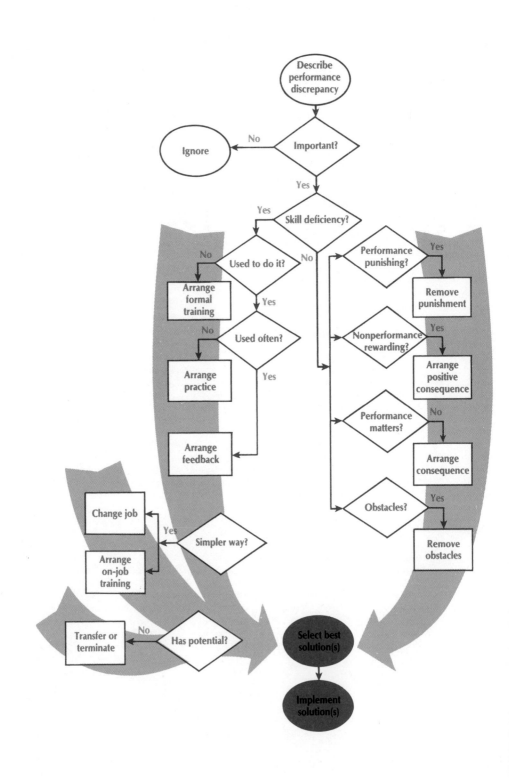

12 || Which Solution Is Best?

■ **WHERE WE ARE**

One or more solutions or remedies for a performance discrepancy have been identified.

Isn't this the end of the line? By now you probably have what looks like one or more relevant solutions, so why not put them to work?

It's true you've cleared most of the hurdles, but there's one more question to ponder before racing for the finish line: Will the results be worth the trouble? This can be a tougher question than it seems, and all too often it doesn't get the attention it deserves.

If you have followed the procedure we've described, you'll have concentrated on finding solutions that are *related* to a problem, without too much regard for whether the solution is the most practical or feasible in your situation. As a result, one or more of the remedies you have generated may be inappropriate simply because they are beyond the resources you can bring to bear. Perhaps it's plain that you would not be able to get the money, perhaps it violates policy, or maybe you don't have the organizational "muscle" to implement it.

So, as the first step in deciding which solution is best, ask these questions of each one:

- Is this possible solution clearly inappropriate or impossible to implement?
- Is this possible solution plainly beyond our resources?

When the answer to either of the questions is yes, put the solution aside for the moment. Don't discard these possibilities, though; someone may be able to show you how to put that "unworkable" solution into practice. Too many "It can't be done" and "It's against company policy" assertions have been shown to be untrue, so avoid being hasty about scrapping solutions that look impossible at first glance.

Determine the "Cost" of Each Solution.   The next step is to determine the "cost" of each of the remaining solutions. Just as you affixed a value to each of the consequences of the discrepancy, now determine what it would cost to adopt each of the tentative solutions you developed during the analysis. Why bother with each one? For two important reasons. (1) All too often, perhaps without realizing it, people lock onto a solution without giving "equal time" to other potential answers. The selected solution may be one they had even before doing the analysis; or it may be one that, on the face of it, is more "obviously" right than others. That's not to say that either of these types of solutions will never be the right one. But plunging too quickly for an answer without considering the cost of all alternatives deprives you of another advantage—the other important reason. (2) As you ponder costs, you will probably find yourself generating even more solutions, compromises, and combinations that are often more innovative and more appropriate than the original answers.

Don't jump too quickly, either, to the conclusion that any solution comes free of cost. Consider, for example, the common problem of instructors who insult or humiliate their students in one way or another (such as forcing them to participate in ill-conceived role-plays).

"There's a discrepancy between what these instructors are doing and what they should be doing," says someone. "We've got to do something about that."

"Fine. How will you get them to stop doing it?"

"Why, we'll *tell* them to stop."

So "telling" is proposed as the solution. And, on the face of it, this solution doesn't cost anything at all. All you have to do is to tell. But it isn't as simple as that, is it? Even if telling worked—which it seldom does— someone has to decide how the telling should happen. Will someone prepare a memo for all instructors? Will someone sit down with them in a group and tell? Or meet with them individually and tell? It is clear that when you think about the proposed solution in terms of "cost," it isn't as free as it looks. It may be quick and easy to do; but even for a solution of such dubious effectiveness, there is likely to be a "cost" in terms of someone's time, at the very least.

It's that way with most solutions. It "costs" somebody something to "do something." Perhaps not much, but something. When considering solutions, then, it is useful to estimate the cost of each tentative action. It will help prevent you from rushing off to implement a solution settled on before the analysis; it will help you to put the "obvious" solution into perspective; and it will help prevent you from implementing solutions that are more massive than the problem. After all, you wouldn't want to find yourself in the position of implementing hundred-thousand-dollar solutions to ten-thousand-dollar problems, or requiring ten people to involve themselves in a solution when a checklist would do as well.

Clearly, money is an important measuring instrument in decisions regarding solutions for performance discrepancies. After all, if you can't afford a particular solution, or if a solution costs more than the results are likely to be worth, plainly there is further analysis to be done. A less obvious case, perhaps, is that of doing nothing. The cost of the solution should be weighed against the cost of maintaining the status quo. What looks at first like an "unreasonable" cost may look considerably more attractive if the true cost of the present situation is examined.

There's a tendency to say that an existing state of affairs "costs nothing" and that any solution that entails an added outlay of money therefore has to be more expensive. But the "hidden cost" of "doing nothing" about a performance discrepancy can be considerable—in inefficient performance, overly long or unnecessary courses, scrap piles larger than they need be, lost or angry customers, employee turnover and absenteeism, and varying degrees of frustration.

Recently, the trainers of a large corporation spent more than a hundred thousand dollars in the development and validation of a single course; a very expensive solution, indeed. But *too* expensive? Hardly. The new course is only *one-fifth* the length of the old one, and it turns out individuals who can perform better than former graduates. The invested dollars are repaid several times over each year.

Intangible Costs.   The paragraphs above may make it sound as though we are talking only about money when estimating solution costs. Not so. There are cost dimensions other than monetary ones, as a proposed solution will often require time, talent, people-dedication, hard work, and so on. These intangibles must not be ignored; and when included in the sum total of the solution requirement, the solution may not be worth the expected results.

Consider for a moment the "problem" of getting people to buckle their seat belts when driving. "People really oughta wanna wear their seat belts," goes the cry. What happens if they *don't*? Statistics are trotted out to "prove" that a certain number of people will die. And how much is a life worth? How much should we be willing to spend to prevent people from dying as a result of their own folly? Clearly, there are intangible costs incurred by letting the problem alone, and some intangible costs incurred by "solving" the problem (costs such as the loss of freedom to act as one wishes and beltburn on the necks of shorter drivers, to mention only two).

In the United States, millions of dollars have been spent on bells, buzzers, interlocks, and widespread exhortation to "buckle up." This expensive "solution" hasn't worked very well. Elsewhere, better results have been achieved almost at the

stroke of a pen. Australia, for example, has passed a law requiring a fine whenever, and for whatever reason, anyone is
caught driving without a fastened seat belt. The result is better
than 85 percent compliance, a far more successful solution
than that of "throwing money at the problem."

But how to evaluate intangible costs? Most of the time it is
easier than it looks. The procedure for evaluating intangible
solution costs is threefold: (1) name the intangibles; (2) describe the components of people and effort that would be
required to implement the solution; and (3) describe the implications of implementation, whether they be political or personal. The use of this procedure may not provide you with
precise numbers, but it will put you in a better position to rank
solutions in terms of total cost.

By the time you have identified an area of intangible costs
and have described the amount of effort that will be involved,
the practicality of the solution may be obvious. For example,
once you see that cleaning up the neighborhood will take the
efforts of 50 volunteers, and that it would take more organiz-
ing and bell-ringing and telephoning hours than you have to
offer, the solution of "get the neighbors to do it" looks pretty
unlikely—even without thinking about monetary aspects of
the cost.

Or consider the plight of the training director of a large
bank.

"We lose about a half million dollars a year through bank
robberies!"

"Sounds like a lot. What do you do about it?"

"Plenty. We hire more guards, we buy cameras and miles
of film, we teach people complex defensive routines, and we
buy other special equipment."

"How much does *that* cost?"

"Don't ask."

"You mean it costs *more* than half a million a year?"

"It sure does."

"Why do it if it costs more than the problem?"

"Well, it has value other than just deterring robberies. Our customers are reassured by knowing we have all the latest gadgets, and we look 'up to date' in the eyes of our peers. We feel that those results, unmeasurable though they may be, make it important to spend more on a solution than the problem is costing."

"Sounds like a wise decision."

"Well, it is and it isn't."

"Oh?"

"Well, we lose half a million a year in robberies, but we lose twenty-four million a year in loan losses."

"Wow! What do you do about *that?*"

"Nothing."

"Nothing?"

"Nothing. Most of that loss is caused by vice-presidents who fail to follow established loan procedure. They make loans against the better judgment established by policy, the loan goes sour, and we lose a bundle."

"Why isn't something done about the problem?"

"Ahh, it's called clout. The board or the president could do something about it, but my department doesn't have the clout. So we concentrate our efforts on the robberies."

(If you think we invented this episode, you're wrong.)

You can probably think of several examples of instances in which the intangible (unmeasurable) costs of the solutions played a large part in the decision on just *which* solution would be tried. Once the intangible costs have been evaluated, the monetary aspect often pales in comparison.

Evaluate Solutions.   Which solution (or combination of solutions) is best? What action should you take? By now it's possible that one solution will stand out clearly as being better than the others you considered. The value of implementing the solution will clearly be positive. The solution will be *economical* (considerably *cheaper* than the problem). It will be *practical*, in that the means for implementing it are available to you. It will be *feasible*, in that it will be acceptable to the people affected and not harmful (politically or otherwise) to you or others.

But what happens if all of your potential solutions are rejected because they were plainly beyond your resources? Or because, on close examination, they proved unfeasible or impractical?

The answer is the same for both. You will have to re-examine the problem and the solution to see if one or both can be scaled down. Ask:

- Can the problem be attacked in parts?
- Can a portion of the solution be used to solve a portion of the problem?

Sometimes it makes good sense to settle for less than the ultimate solution. If you shoot for something less than perfection, you may be able to get acceptable results for a good deal less effort. Or, when problems and solutions seem out of reach, it often makes sense to ask: What will give us the most result for the least effort? Which aspect are we best equipped to tackle? Which part of the problem interests us most? Which part of the problem is the most "visible" to those who must be pleased? So . . .

- If you can't afford to train 50 people, can you train five and have them provide on-the-job training for their colleagues?
- If you can't afford to hire all the guards indicated for plant security, can you shore things up sufficiently with closed-circuit TV?
- If you don't have room in the house for a piano, could your child learn to play the piccolo?
- If you don't have the room or the teachers in your school to provide vital vocational training, can you persuade local industry to provide some space and know-how?
- If you can't provide the service to *all*, can you find a quick way to tell who needs the service most?

- If you can't find a foolproof way of telling whether ammunition is in working order other than by firing it, can you use a random sampling technique that will be almost as good?

In summary, answer the "What do I do now?" question by: (a) identifying as many potential solutions as possible, (b) making sure that the solutions address the issues revealed by your analysis (such as the need to reduce punishment of desired performance or the need to eliminate obstacles), (c) determining or estimating the cost of implementing each solution, and (d) selecting the solution(s) that will add the most value (solve the largest part of the problem for the least effort).

What to Do

Estimate the cost of each potential solution and select the solution or combination of solutions that is most practical, feasible, and economical.

How to Do It

Answer these questions:

- *Have all the potential solutions been identified?*
- *Does each solution address itself to one or more problems identified during the analysis (such as skill deficiency, absence of potential, incorrect rewards, punishing consequences, distracting obstacles)?*
- *What is the cost of each potential solution?*
- *Have the intangible (unmeasurable) costs been assessed?*
- *Which solution is most practical, feasible, and economical?*
- *Which solution will add most value (solve the largest part of the problem for the least effort)?*
- *Which remedy is likely to give us the most result for the least effort?*
- *Which solution are we best equipped to try?*
- *Which remedy interests us most? (Or, on the other side of the coin, which remedy is most visible to those who must be pleased?)*

PART

V

Quick-Reference Checklist

Now that the steps of our performance analysis are familiar to you, we can give them to you in a quick-reference checklist. Use the checklist as a guide or as a way to help others see why they really oughta wanna re-evaluate solutions they have already decided upon.

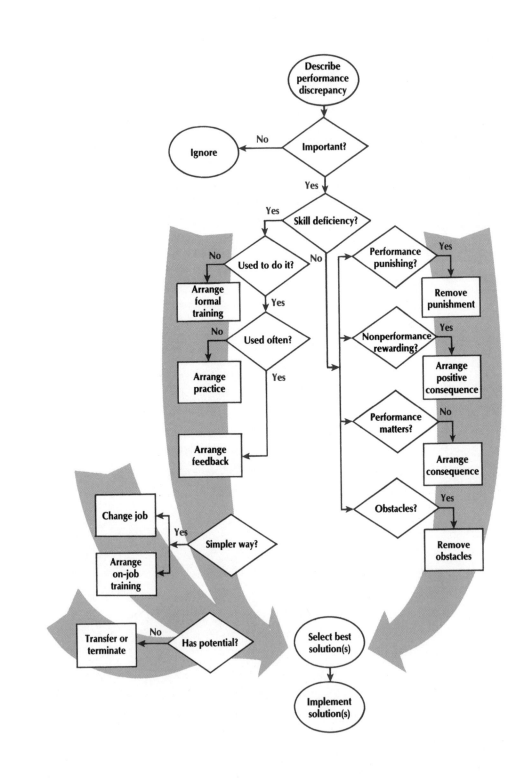

QUICK-REFERENCE CHECKLIST

KEY QUESTIONS TO ANSWER	PROBE QUESTIONS
I. They're not doing what they should be doing. *I think I've got a training problem.*	
1. What is the performance discrepancy?	• Why do I think there is a training problem? • What is the difference between what is being done and what is supposed to be done? • What is the event that causes me to say that things aren't right? • Why am I dissatisfied?
2. Is it important?	• Why is the discrepancy important? (What is its cost?) • What would happen if I left the discrepancy alone? • Could doing something to resolve the discrepancy have any worthwhile result?
3. Is it a skill deficiency?	• Could the person do it if really required to do it? • Could the person do it if his or her life depended on it? • Are the person's present skills adequate for the desired performance?

KEY QUESTIONS TO ANSWER	PROBE QUESTIONS
II. Yes. It is a skill deficiency. *They couldn't do it if their lives depended on it.*	
4. Could they do it in the past?	• Did the person once know how to perform as desired? • Has the person forgotten how to do what I want done?
5. Is the skill used often?	• How often is the skill or performance used? • Is there regular feedback on performance? • Exactly how does the person find out how well he or she is doing?
6. Is there a simpler solution?	• Can I change the job by providing some kind of job aid? • Can I store the needed information some way (in written instructions, checklists) other than in someone's head? • Can I show rather than train? • Would informal (such as on-the-job) training be sufficient?
7. Do they have what it takes?	• Could the person learn the job (is the individual trainable)? • Does this person have the physical and mental potential to perform as desired? • Is this person overqualified for the job?

KEY QUESTIONS TO ANSWER	PROBE QUESTIONS
III. It is not a skill deficiency. *They could do it if they wanted to.*	
8. Is desired performance punishing?	• What is the consequence of performing as desired? • Is it punishing to perform as expected? • Does the person perceive desired performance as being geared to penalties? • Would the person's world become a little dimmer if the desired performance were attained?
9. Is nonperformance rewarding?	• What is the result of doing it the present way instead of my way? • What does the person get out of the present performance in the way of reward, prestige, status, jollies? • Does the person get more attention for misbehaving than for behaving? • What event in the world supports (rewards) the present way of doing things? (Am I inadvertently rewarding irrelevant behavior while overlooking the crucial behaviors?) • Is this person "mentally inadequate," doing less so that there is less to worry about?

KEY QUESTIONS TO ANSWER	PROBE QUESTIONS
	• Is this person physically inadequate, doing less because it is less tiring?
10. Does performing really matter to them?	• Does performing as desired matter to the performer? • Is there a favorable outcome for performing? • Is there an undesirable outcome for not performing? • Is there a source of satisfaction for performing? • Can the person take pride in this performance as an individual or as a member of a group? • Is there satisfaction of personal needs from the job?

11. Are there obstacles to performing?	• What prevents this person from performing?
	• Does the person know what is expected?
	• Does the person know when to do what is expected?
	• Are there conflicting demands on this person's time?
	• Does the person lack
	    . . . the authority?
	    . . . the time?
	    . . . the tools?
	• Are there restrictive policies, or a "right way of doing it," or a "way we've always done it" that ought to be changed?

KEY QUESTIONS TO ANSWER	PROBE QUESTIONS
	• Can I reduce interference by . . . improving lighting? . . . changing colors? . . . increasing comfort? . . . modifying the work position? . . . reducing visual or auditory distractions? • Can I reduce "competition from the job"—phone calls, "brush fires," demands of less important but more immediate problems?

IV. What should I do now?

12. Which solution is best?	• Have all the potential solutions been identified? • Does each solution address itself to one or more problems identified during the analysis (such as skill deficiency, absence of potential, incorrect rewards, punishing consequences, distracting obstacles)? • What is the cost of each potential solution? • Have the intangible (unmeasurable) costs been assessed? • Which solution is most practical, feasible, and economical? • Which solution will add most value (solve the largest part of the problem for the least effort)?

KEY QUESTIONS TO ANSWER	PROBE QUESTIONS
	• Which remedy is likely to give us the most result for the least effort?
	• Which solution are we best equipped to try?
	• Which remedy interests us most? (Or, on the other side of the coin, which remedy is most visible to those who must be pleased?)

Epilogue

We have described in this book a way of analyzing a particular kind of problem—that of human performance. Though it may seem to have taken a long time to describe it, it doesn't take long to *use* it. The procedure, after all, represents a way of thinking about things; and, after a little practice, you will find yourself quickly ticking your mental way through the key questions. In just a few seconds you will be able to see a problem in a new light—and then point to a solution that's likely to work.

If you analyze *your* performance problems systematically, you may even come to view some of the larger problems of the world from a new vantage point and understand why some of the "tried and true" solutions are so ineffective. You may, for example, find new ways of thinking and responding to such comments as:

"Politicians oughta wanna reduce government spending."

"Posters hung in public places will help reduce the incidence of traffic deaths."

"The Russians oughta wanna stop being aggressive."

"Industry oughta wanna stop hiring illegal aliens."

"People oughta wanna make the government obey the Constitution."

Our checklist won't help you to understand *everything* about why people behave as they do. Nothing will do that . . . yet. But if each of us could perceive more clearly the nature of just *one* important human problem—and throw his or her weight behind a solution *related* to the cause—we might just move bigger and more important things than mountains.

It's worth trying.

Reprisal!

Every book should have a little corner from which authors are allowed to strike back. After all, several dozen individuals have had a go at our thoughts and at our manuscript—picking and probing, suggesting this, trampling on that, or just staring blankly at a mangled explanation they really should have understood.

Such knavery cannot go unsung—so sing we will. We wave the banner of acclaim for all those who so patiently allowed themselves to be battered by earlier, more primitive explanations of the concepts presented herein, and who were magnanimous enough to batter back.

More pointedly, we skewer with the lance of laud and commendation these generous souls who took pains to try on one or another of our later drafts and tell us just where it pinched and how the fit could be improved: John McCann, Rodney Cron, Randy Mager, Maryjane Rees, Vernon Rees, Andy Stevens, Walter Thorne, and Tom Watts.

Long may they dangle!

Robert F. Mager
Peter Pipe

For Your
Further Reading...

Gilbert, Thomas F. *Human Competence: Engineering Worthy Performance.* New York: McGraw-Hill Book Co., 1978.

Zemke, R. *Figuring Things Out.* Reading, Mass.: Addison-Wesley Publishing Co., 1982.